A Light at the End of the Tunnel:
Guiding you Through the Federal Prison System

There is no information like inside information

As told by Former Inmates

Written by James Kelleher

James Kelleher

A Light At the End of the Tunnel

Guiding You Through the Federal Prison System

Print ISBN: 978-1-48356-888-1
eBook ISBN: 978-1-48356-889-8

TABLE OF CONTENTS

ACKNOWLEDGEMENTS

I would like to acknowledge the following wonderful people for their contributions to this book. Without their help this book would not have been possible.

First and foremost, my Mom, Patricia, who has always had my back, and whose never-ending love and support has helped me through this prison term. My family, whose support and understanding made surviving this experience possible. To my boys in room 313 at FCI Fort Dix (Westside)--just sending a shout out.

A special thanks to Chris and Fran for all they have done for me.

There were so many people who stuck by me and prayed for me. I am grateful for my friend Jodi who continues to be there for me.

To John M. thank you for creating my website and for your help and guidance along the way.

To my good friends George and Ira, thanks for guiding me through the technical aspects of publishing this book, and for added insight into getting this book off the ground and completed.

At one of the lowest points of my entire life I was lucky enough to meet a man that believes in me, supports me and became a true friend to me. Thank you Leo and family for all of your support.

To my boy Keith (Keeba) for all of the substantial financial assistance and online research that you have provided me. You believed in me when others didn't.

And to a very special person...you know who you are; I couldn't have come this far without your love and support.

This book is also dedicated to Jim and John, two brothers who have always treated me as family. I will spend the rest of my life apologizing for the hurt I have caused them and their families. I love you guys with all my heart.

INTRODUCTION

Hello, my name is Jimbo K. While serving federal time at Lewisburg Federal Camp, my friend and I were discussing how much easier the transition to entering prison would have been if information was available. I served a federal sentence of 60 months for a federal drug charge for selling less than 5 kilos of cocaine. My friend has organized crime ties and is serving a 22 year sentence for bank fraud, money laundering, and loan sharking activities. He has served 17 years and has been to Otisville, NY (Medium), and FCI Lows at Fort Dix, NJ, Safford, and Ashland. He finally worked his way down to a camp. With the RDAP program, his journey back to freedom began in January 2015. Based on our true life experiences, this book will provide you with detailed and expert advice on easing your transition into incarceration. You will have a heads up on the do's and don'ts while serving time, and be more informed. We hope you enjoy the book.

It is not rare in today's troubled times to know a relative or a friend who is presently incarcerated. The United States has 7% of the world's population, but 25% of which are presently incarcerated. Since 9/11, the Feds have picked up nickel and dime cases that had previously been strictly in the States' domain. However, since the states rely on evidence and not hearsay, they subsequently lost numerous cases that went to trial. The Feds, on the other hand, will indict a ham and cheese sandwich. It is easier for them to use hearsay of two corroborating witnesses to send you to the slammer. You can go to jail for life if the two witnesses make up lies about you even if there is not a single shred of evidence. Feds have a 97% conviction rate and will double your time if you do not take a plea agreement, and subsequently, blow trial. They penalize you for spending tax dollars and having them work for your conviction. Now more than ever you can easily get hooked in a federal investigation which brings a federal indictment. With international terrorism looming at our borders, the United States has become somewhat of a police state.

The purpose of this book is to inform recently convicted federal inmates what they should expect once they begin to serve their federal sentences. This information is priceless. It will ease the transition of anyone entering the federal system for the first time. It will give you a head start in serving your time and steer you away from the negative forces that seem to take hold once despair and depression set in. I know you feel as though your entire world is crashing around you and you have all of these crazy thoughts running through your head. I can tell you that running away is not an option, there is no place to run to these days plus they will add years to your sentence. You wouldn't be able to call or email your family ever again. Or the other thought you are having is I won't ever be able to survive prison, but you are wrong you will and you will come out the other end a much better person. Make sure you read this book until you know it cover to cover. This will make your transition to prison a whole lot easier, you will know what is going to happen before it happens and it is always better to not allow yourself to be blindsided. YOU WILL GET THROUGH THIS.

Remember "Club Fed, you're not invited unless you are indicted". LOL

Sincerely,

Jimbo K.

DEFINITIONS

Official Terms

<u>A & O</u> – Admissions and orientation – Each inmate gets schooled in the rules and regulations of that institution upon arrival.

<u>ACE</u> – Adult Continuing Education program is sponsored by the educational department of the Federal facility where you reside. They have continuing education programs that you can take to learn a trade, self-educate, and ease yourself upon reentry into society.

<u>Appeals</u> – When you wish an objective decision on your case from an appellate panel. Sometimes, your presiding judge or lawyer made an error that you wish to correct. If this error is found to be in your favor, you can get a time reduction or immediate release.

<u>Arraignment</u> – A court hearing where the individual accused can plead guilty or not guilty to the indictment of charges the prosecutor presented to the presiding judge.

<u>AW</u> – Assistant Warden

<u>Bail</u> – After the arraignment, the defendant can request bail. With bail, the defendant can fight his case from the outside. He or she can attend court from the street. Usually, bail requires either property, cash, or signatures from friends and relatives. This somewhat ensures that you won't skip town and risk the loss of the assets of loved ones. It is also very important to obtain bail rather than fight your case from behind bars, where your movements are restricted.

BOP – Stands for Bureau of Prisons; responsible for the welfare of inmates residing in the Federal prison system.

Cadre – Refers to a person's work detail comprised of inmates who have community custody "camp status" and can travel freely in an institutional setting without creating havoc. For example, in Brooklyn's Federal Detention Center, they have a cadre of inmates assigned there who are camp status and already sentenced. They are put to work in the kitchen and maintenance areas of that facility because they can travel freely from floor to floor of a tightly controlled institution.

Callouts – Are available every day just before or after the 4:00 pm count. They are the next day's scheduled appointments for inmates on that compound only. You must check the callout list for appointments that you may have (e.g. medical callouts for treatment or evaluation and/or education callouts for a new class that you signed up for). Failure to attend your callouts will lead to a disciplinary shot.

Case Manager – He/she monitors your progress and is responsible for your transfers to lower level facilities and halfway house time. He/she is basically your coach and mentor while you are in custody.

CIM – Central Inmate Monitor – This is when inmates have codefendants in the system that they are not allowed to be with. Either the government is afraid they can gather and commit more crime, or maybe one codefendant ratted on the other, and is a risk factor that has to be controlled.

Classification – Your custody and security scoring indicates the security facility level that you must be held in. If you constantly get in trouble and receive shots, your scoring will rise and may include a transfer to a tougher prison. However, if you stay out of trouble and take rehabilitative programs to help yourself, your case manager has the power to lower your points and send you to a Federal "prison camp".

<u>CO</u> – Correctional Officer – responsible for the daily health and activities of inmates at that institution.

<u>Commissary</u> – A store inside the prison where inmates on certain days and times can purchase food, toiletries, and clothes.

<u>Compound</u> – Refers to the prison's entire physical boundaries. It includes the administrative buildings, chow hall, education, UNICOR, and housing units.

<u>Cop-out</u> – A form that inmates use to advise staff of an issue that needs to be addressed. Staff has 48 hours to respond and must do so in writing.

This term is also used when the prosecutor believes he/she has enough evidence to convict you of your pending charges and would rather save the time and expense of going to trial. The advantage to a cop-out agreement is the government usually reduces your time as an incentive not to go to trial.

<u>CORRLINKS</u> – allows you to send emails to friends and family from a Federal correctional institution provided you are approved for access and the receiving party accepts.

<u>Count Times</u> – Every institution conducts counts to confirm attendance and to make sure no one escapes. The main count for the Feds is at 4:00 PM each day. The 4:00 PM count is phoned into Washington daily. Messing the count up is not a good idea and can get you a shot, if not directly placed into the SHU. At count time, you must be properly dressed, no radio on, and standing by your bunk. You cannot leave that area until count is cleared. Count times during the week are 12 AM, 3 AM, 5 AM, 4 PM, 10 PM. Weekends are 12 AM, 3 AM,

5 AM, 10 AM, 4 PM, and 10 PM. Some counts are a standing count and you must stand up until the CO counts you.

Custody Levels – Pertain to an individual's classification of custody based on violence, inmate history, and the seriousness of the crime itself.

DHO – Disciplinary Hearing Officer – responsible for sentencing all disciplinary shots at level 100 or 200. Also, if an inmate receives 2 or more level 300 shots, the CO has the option to refer that inmate's sentencing to the DHO. Inmates usually refer to him as the Grim Reaper since he usually gives severe penalties to inmates for their bad behavior.

DTS – Drug Treatment Specialist

Extra Duty – Sometimes when an inmate is caught doing something wrong, the CO can offer the inmate extra duty to fulfill his punishment if it was a minor incident or if that inmate is usually in good standing.

FRP – Financial Responsibility Program – A program designed to help inmates pay their court costs, restitution, child support, or other financial payments the court has brought against them.

Furlough – When an inmate is allowed to travel freely to another institution or home without Federal or state supervision.

Halfway House – Upon the near completion of your time physically incarcerated, you may be eligible for halfway house time. Halfway house refers to your placement back into society with

supervision. You get situated and return to the community, look for a job and are allowed to get weekend furloughs to visit your family. Freedom begins here. You must adhere to the rules, you can get disciplinary shots that will violate your halfway house time and send you back to prison.

<u>High</u> – A high level of custody based on the length of an inmate's time and his potential for violence which may require a higher level of supervision, hence the placement in a high facility.

<u>Indicted</u> – The process of being charged for a criminal action by the state or Federal government. A grand jury of your peers must find enough evidence against you for the prosecutor to proceed against you. If the grand jury issues the indictment, then a warrant is officially issued for your arrest.

<u>ITS</u> – Inmate Telephone System <u>Google Voice</u> – Is a telephone service by Google that allows inmates to save substantial monthly telephone expenses by changing their most frequently called phone numbers to local area codes where they are presently incarcerated. For example, a local call costs 6 cents per minute, while the BOP charges 23 cents per minute for non-local phone numbers. The total minutes an inmate receives are 300 per month. So an inmate can save fifty to sixty dollars per month by using Google Voice to localize their most frequent phone numbers.

<u>J&C</u> – A legal document called Judgment and Commitment. It states the prisoner's charges, counts and sums up the amount of time that must be served. It also states if an individual received a Federal sentence below the guidelines. This indicates that he cooperated 90% of the time if his sentence falls below the original guideline range. Many inmates want to see your J&C for that purpose.

<u>Lockdowns</u> - A lockdown is when an institution limits the daily normal movement activities of inmates in order to investigate a potential problem, or something that has already happened.

<u>Low</u> – Minimum custody level. A lot of movement and freedom. Inmate profile is less violent and the seriousness of the crime merits placement here.

<u>Main Line</u> – The afternoon lunch meal at a Federal facility. At main line, all levels of staff representing all areas of that institution are available to hear any pertinent issues you may have or have been unable to resolve. At main line, the Warden and Assistant Warden are available as well. However, remember you should respect the chain of command when looking to resolve your problems. You don't want to upset a staff member who has been assigned to handle your daily problems. If you go over their head and you get in trouble, you might find yourself on the first bus out of there. "Diesel Therapy"

<u>Medium Federal Facility</u> – A Medium Federal Facility has a lower security than a penitentiary, but a higher level than a low facility. To be placed in a medium FCI, your points must be in the 15-20 point range. Most criminal cases that are considered to have an element of violence cause the inmate to be designated to a medium destination. As time passes, the inmate can work himself down to a low facility if he programs and his behavior is good. If an inmate at a medium acts badly, he can see his points rise and be transferred to a higher facility which is more dangerous and secure.

<u>Military Time</u> – You need to know this: All you do is subtract 12 hours – so if the time is 13:30, you just subtract the 12 hours, which means the time is 1:30 pm

<u>OC </u>– Organized crime

<u>OTC </u>– Over the counter

<u>Orderlies </u>– Unit orderlies are responsible for maintaining a clean environment in the unit. They clean the bathrooms and kill germs which can spread among the large number of inmates using

those bathrooms. You can become either a unit orderly or work as an orderly doing the same duties at FCIs various educational and medical facilities.

Pedophile – Term used to classify a sexual offender involved with the abuse of minors of a pornographic or physical nature.

Penitentiary – A maximum security facility where there is a lot of violence and where rats, chomos, and homos are not tolerated. Respect level is high but a lot of these inmates are doing life or a substantial amount of time.

PA – Physician's Assistant

Parolee – Someone who is not incarcerated but under Federal supervision to make sure he walks a straight line.

Plea Agreement – A formal agreement by the prosecutor and the defendant agreeing to certain charges and the time associated with them.

Probation – A period of time when your movements after you leave jail are supervised.

Probation Officer – Someone who monitors your behavior upon release from prison.

Prosecutor – The person who is pursuing your conviction either by plea agreement or by trial.

Public Safety Factor – A term staff uses and places on an individual to limit his movement to a lower security level than he could normally qualify for. For example, an individual like a pedophile cannot go to a camp in the BOP because he has a public safety factor issue concerning the potential danger to the community he goes to without the proper notification and help that may not have been completed at that time prior to his release.

PSR/PSI – A detailed report completed by the Probation Office. They provide the judge with a list of the charges against you and your personal family history.

R & D – Receiving and Departures – Inmates are processed here when they arrive or leave the prison for either writs, go back to court, release to a halfway house, or any other Federal custody transfer.

RDAP – Residential Drug Abuse Program – a 9 to 12 month program which helps to rehabilitate inmates who have drug or alcohol abuse issues. Completion of the program entitles some participants to receive extra good-time credit.

Register Number – Every Federal inmate receives a number so they can be identified among other prisoners.

Remanded – The process of leaving court and surrendering your freedom by entering Federal or state custody. For example, you might be arrested and after your arraignment, bail is denied and the judge remands you to Federal custody. At that time you are going to either a county or Federal detention center to begin fighting your case from the inside.

Revalidation – Based on the 5th number of your register number, times 3 plus 1. Every month your spending limit for commissary and limit on telephone minutes resets back to three hundred twenty to three hundred forty dollars and 300 minutes per month. For example, if your Register Number is xxxx2-047, your revalidation date would be 2 X 3 = 6 + 1 = 7. On the 7th of each month you revalidate.

PAC – Your personal number which is needed to make personal phone calls and to use the TRULINCS email system.

Sentencing Procedures – The formal process of listing all facts and mitigating circumstances of an individual's guilt. The way these facts are reviewed will impact the length of an inmate's formal sentence and judgment.

Shakedown – A process where the COs remove the inmates from their housing quarters and search for contraband, weapons, and drugs.

Shower Shoes – They are a must before you step into any institutional shower. You must buy them or ask another inmate upon your arrival if a Christian group is organized there. The Christian group usually has a care package for new inmates upon their arrival. The care package has basic toiletries and usually you just have to replace it when you have a chance to go to commissary.

Shots - A shot is given to an inmate when he is caught by a CO or staff member doing a prohibited act. For example, if someone is caught stealing from the kitchen, he can receive a disciplinary shot for that.

SHU – Special Housing Unit – Where inmates are sent to when they commit a serious, prohibited act and are a danger to the general population of the prison.

Team – The term is used when an inmate confers with his unit team. This occurs once every six months until the inmate has under a year left on his sentence, then it becomes once every three months.

Trial – The process of presenting your case or plea of innocence to a jury of your peers who will listen to all of the evidence presented by the prosecutor and your defense lawyer. When the trial is finished, you will either be set free or found guilty of certain charges and then must await a formal sentencing hearing.

TRULINCS – The term used for the Federal system's new computer access service. TRULINCS must be used for your mail service. TRULINCS are charged at a rate of 5 cents per TRULINC unit. TRULINCS also needs to be purchased if you want to purchase songs for your MP3 player.

UNICOR – UNICOR is where inmates can do industrial work for better working pay. The industries are usually located at that facility. You get to make up to one hundred to two hundred dollars per month. You earn vacation and sick day pay and have the option to work overtime when available. Inmates with substantial fines are sometimes required to work there. There is a formal procedure to apply for a UNICOR job. At A & O orientation, you can express your interest in that opportunity if you so desire.

Unit Team – Refers to an inmate's counselor, case manager, and unit manager. These people guide that inmate by advising him how to utilize the program and rehabilitate back into society. They also handle any other problems individuals may have.

Warden – He/she is the big cheese of that institution. He/she determines policies of that institution and sets the overall tone of that facility. If he/she is easy going, for example, it usually trickles down to the attitude of the COs.

Slang Terms

<u>190</u> – Hot water

<u>5%-ers</u> – Inmates who believe they are gods

<u>Action</u> – When you bet on sports

<u>Bidding Off Someone</u> – You hang with an inmate who is crazy or funny to make your time go faster.

<u>Bed Roll</u> – All of your bedding (sheets, blanket, pillow, pillow case)

<u>Blew Up</u> – When you bet on sports and a team made you lose, the ticket blew up.

<u>Blow Trial</u> – A term inmates use when they lose at trial and will most likely receive a harsher sentence for rejecting the earlier plea agreement.

<u>Bullpen</u> - Refers to the holding cells prisoners must sit in until they are processed to enter prison population and be formally processed.

<u>Bunk Roll</u> – When you arrive at prison a bunk roll will be given to you. It consists of 2 sheets, 2 blankets, 2 towels and a pillow.

<u>Bunkie</u> – The person you share your cube or bunk bed with

<u>Cars</u> – Simply indicates the place an inmate belongs based on his geographic or racial profiles. The car stands for that group's unity in dealing with other inmate's problems or issues.

<u>Cellie</u> – Person or persons you live with

<u>Cheese Factory</u> - A term inmates use to describe a prison or building where cooperating inmates are housed. They are not allowed to be in general population because their safety will be

compromised. Usually these cheese factories are reserved for rats who are high profile and targeted for revenge by power syndicates like the mafia, drug cartels, and gangs.

Chomo – The term inmates use to refer to pedophiles and child molesters.

Clipping Your Claws – Clipping your nails; always do this over a garbage can.

Come Up – Something you get cheaper than it is worth

Coming Down – The COs are walking and doing the counts.

Cooperating – The process of inmates helping the prosecutor with the details of their crime or the details of crimes of others. These inmates cooperate to obtain a 5K cooperation agreement which will limit their time behind bars, or let them go free immediately after completion of plea agreements or trials of people he helped indict.

Crackhead Soup – Ramen noodle soup

Crash Dummy – Someone you can send to do something stupid and take the fall for it.

Crop Dusting – An inmate farting and walking around

Cum Jumpers – Another name for shower shoes

Detainer - A detainer is when an inmate has another unresolved legal case pending against him. It prohibits the movement of an inmate to a minimum camp status because they do not understand how serious that unresolved matter may be.

Diesel Therapy – The terms inmates and BOP staff members use when they send a particular problem inmate across the country and move him constantly from jail to jail so he can't get situated comfortably.

Down in Front – Means you are standing in front of the TV and they can't see through you.

Drop a Dime – to tell or rat on someone else.

Dropping Notes – When an inmate tells on you and slips a note under the door of a COs office

Dropping the Warden Off – Taking a shit.

DU – Dirty urine

Ear Hustling – Refers to the terms of listening to someone else's conversation. This is a no-no and could lead to a fight if the conversation was meant to be private in nature. Those people might think that you are going to snitch on them. Do not ear hustle and mind your own business.

First Time Buy – When an inmate arrives at his final prison destination, he can shop on the first available day of commissary. He does not have to wait until his assigned day.

Foot on his Neck – Keeping pressure on someone.

Getting in Someone's Lane – You are minding someone else's business – don't do this.

Getting it in – If someone is sleeping or snoring, they will say that he is getting it in.

Getting Money – When you are working out or getting ready to work out.

Gump – Gay Until Making Parole

Hammer/Jack/Joint – Telephone

Hemmed Up – This is a term an inmate uses when his actions have caught up with him, and he is against the wall. For example, he runs up a big store bill thinking his people are sending him money and something happens where they can't. He now has to explain the situation to a thirsty and mad store guy.

<u>Herb</u> – someone who won't defend himself

<u>Home Jail</u> – that is what you call the prison you are at where you will be serving your sentence.

<u>Inmate.com</u> – Information from inmates, most of the time it is not even close to the truth

<u>Jacking Rec</u> – Not giving or allowing you time for sports or working out

<u>Jail House Lawyer</u> – An inmate who can help you with legal advice or paperwork.

<u>Jodi</u> – The guy who's sleeping with your girl after you're in prison

<u>Kite</u> – When an inmate drops a letter or message from another inmate to you or from you.

<u>Knocking the Chow Table</u> – means respect and enjoy your meal

<u>Lock it in</u> – When you hit or bump fists, you locked in your deal or bet

<u>Locks in Socks</u> – Inmates put their locks in their socks and use it as a weapon.

<u>Loose</u> – Not being careful or not caring about what happens.

<u>Mackerels/Stamps</u> – In prison, we are not allowed to have currency for obvious reasons. However, the inmates have established a currency system among themselves so that they can barter for goods and services. For example, macs, tunas, and stamps are given certain dollar value. You may want to buy an extra piece of chicken from someone in the kitchen; the price is one tuna or two macs if it is fried. Obviously, people also can purchase items from other inmates

by buying them commissary items they may want on your shopping day. I think it is a good idea when you arrive at your prison to buy 100 macs or a couple of books of stamps. Kitchen people and people who have hustles generate a lot of macs, tunas and stamps. They are always looking to get rid of them for cash. Be careful when sending money to someone's books or by holding too much "compound cash". It can be taken during a shakedown if you don't have receipts.

Mail Call – The CO is handing out the mail. You must be present to receive it or wait until the next day. You must have your ID with you.

Man Up – 'Fess up to what you did or said

Maytag Man – A guy who does laundry for mackerels for inmates.

Merry Go Round – Paperwork that needs to get signed when you are processing out to go home. Several COs need to sign this.

No Good/Hot – Means that an inmate ratted or snitched, and the COs are watching him.

No Sharks in the Water – By stating this you are telling an inmate that it has been awhile since they showered.

OG – Original gangster or old gangster

Out of Bounds – Indicates where inmates are not allowed to pass through or loiter. For example, the perimeter of the prison has an area closest to the fence that is prohibited.

Out of Pocket – You are out of line

Packed Out – The CO is gathering your stuff to go to the SHU or another prison

Pause – You say pause when you or someone else says some gay shit.

Photo Tickets – Bought in commissary for one dollar.

Pointman/Lookout – Someone watching for COs.

POP OFF – A fight about to happen

Pounding Fists – Always use your right hand, or say "sorry" if you use your left hand…respect.

Pre-Trial – An inmate who is not yet sentenced is considered pre-trial status.

Put You on Blast – To tell the truth about you

PV – Parole violator

Reusables – Everything in prison get reused

Ride with You – That person is going to do the same as you

Riding Dirty – You are walking around with contraband on you.

Rip – Right from the start

Runner – The guy that runs out for packages that are full of contraband.

Self- Surrender – The process of driving to prison with your family on the day your sentence begins.

Shark – An inmate who is looking for someone weak to prey on and take advantage of any way he can.

Shot Caller – The person who is in charge of that race of inmates. For example, Whites, Blacks, Spanish and Jews have a boss who presides over problems an individual in their group may have with an individual from another group. Instead of rioting or involving the COs, the shot callers get together, review the facts and make a decision as to how the problem can be properly corrected.

Short Timer – An inmate with a short sentence

Sick Call – An institutional policy and procedure where inmates can seek medical attention.

Skittles – Slang for anti-psychotic medications

Skinner – is a chomo/rapist

Skunked – When you are playing a sport or cards and get shutout.

Sneak Thieves - Someone who steals from another inmate

Soda Guy – Sells ice cold soda; three for two to three dollars.

Spinning You – Expression used when a counselor is just telling you what you want to hear.

Stinger – A cord that is plugged into a socket then dropped in water to cook the water.

Store – Commissary

Store Guy – A guy that sells commissary to you until your store date, for a price.

Strap Up/Lace Up – Putting on your boots or sneakers to go get into a fight

Test Ya /Push Up On You – If you don't belong to a car to protect you, inmates are going to test ya; which means they will come up to you and see if you are willing to fight or be a pushover. If you are not willing to fight, be prepared to start handing everything over to them, and it won't stop. If you fight back, that shit won't happen anymore and they will move on to the next new guy. So fight back – win, lose or draw, in the long run you'll be glad that you did.

The Bubble – The COs Headquarters

Throw a Jacket on Someone – This is a term that inmates use when someone throws a label on another inmate without having the actual facts of the situation. For example, someone might label a new inmate a pedophile based solely on his geeky looks or demeanor. This is wrong to do.

<u>Throw you Under the Bus</u> – To tell on someone in front of another person.

<u>Uptop </u>– The hole or SHU

<u>Viking</u> – You are a dirty person

<u>Vouch</u> – To back up what someone says

<u>Writ </u>– Going back to court

CHAPTER 1

Indicted

Okay, you have been indicted by a grand jury. The next step is that the Federal District in which the crime took place will issue a warrant for your arrest. The FBI will be knocking at your door very early (5 to 6 am) to ensure that you are home. They may also have a search warrant to inspect your home and/or office looking for evidence to solidify their case against you. Remember the search warrant specifically states which rooms or areas they are allowed to search for evidence. For example, if the search warrant does not include your garage, they can't go in the garage and secure evidence against you. That would be illegal and you should inform your lawyer about this so it can be excluded from your discovery should you go to trial.

Arraignment

After you are arrested you will be brought into District Court for an arraignment. An arraignment is where the Assistant United States Attorney will present the indictment to you and ask you to plead guilty or not guilty. You will plead not guilty to these charges no matter what, even if you are caught in the act with your hand in the cookie jar. At the arraignment, they will usually appoint a lawyer to you to assist in the present legal proceedings. After arraignment, you can request a bail hearing. Being granted bail is very important. You may have to put up property, cash, or obtain the signatures of various individuals to obtain bail bond. Bail allows you to go back home and fight your case from the street. It is always easier to fight your case when you are at home. You will have time to select a good attorney who specializes in the type of crime you are charged with. Also, at your leisure, you can review the evidence or discovery against you and decide whether or not you want to cop-out to a guilty plea, or go to trial if the evidence is sketchy or weak.

Remanded

Remanded means that your bail was denied. There are many reasons why your bail could be denied. These include the severity of the crime, did it contain violent acts or implied threats? Are you a citizen of the United States? They might feel that you're a flight risk because the charges are quite serious and carry a lot of time. It may be the amount of bail was so excessive that it would take time to secure the necessary bail amount. The Feds are notorious for doing this. They do not like it when the Judge grants bail so they will portray what a villain and danger to the community you would be if allowed to go home and fight your case. So let's say you are remanded and denied bail you will be locked-up in a bullpen and wait to be processed at a Federal Detention Center or sent to a local county jail the Feds have contracted with to handle the overflow of Federal inmates, or to separate co-defendants who may decide to cooperate with the Government.

When you arrive at either destination, there are things you must do to ensure your safety and well-being. First, contact your family and let them know where you are. Then have them send you money via Western Union or a postal money order. The prisons have weekly commissary days when you can buy hygiene products, clothing, and food for your daily comfort. You also need money on your account to make telephone calls. We will address commissary, phone calls, and money transfers in later chapters.

At the point after your arrest, you are considered to be in pre-trial status. That means that you will either be taking a guilty plea and agree to a specific amount of time, or go to trial if your lawyer believes the evidence against you is weak.

If you are remanded, your first goal is searching for an attorney who you can afford and who is a specialist in handling the criminal activity that you have been charged with. If you can't afford a lawyer, one will be appointed to you by the Judge at a later proceeding. The most important thing to remember is never discuss the specifics of your case with anyone. The inmates housed with you are looking for any angle to reduce their sentence. There have been many cases where an inmate confides in another inmate about the intricate details of his case, hoping that his newly found friend could help him. Instead, his friend memorizes the details of the case and calls his lawyer. He informs his lawyer that he gathered critical information about your case and is looking to cash in his "Get Out of Jail Free" card. Also, in some cases, these friends lie and tell the prosecutor assigned to your case that you admitted to them that you committed the actual criminal act.

Nowadays, so many people don't think twice about cooperating against their own family and best friends. What makes you think that you share a special relationship or bond with the inmate you just met?

Self-Surrender

If you are lucky enough to walk out of court after you are sentenced, make the most of it. The Judge considers your crime and risk of flight minimal. He is allowing you time to get your affairs in order so you should use this time productively. You will be sent a letter from BOP's Grand Prairie, Texas Designation Center telling you where and what time you are to self-surrender. During this time, take care of any and all medical issues you have. For example, you may have a root canal problem or corrective surgery already scheduled. Get this done NOW. The BOP will not perform any surgeries at their cost when you enter prison unless it is life threatening or necessary (e.g. torn knee ligaments). Carefully document any and all chronic health conditions you may have, including but not limited to: diabetes, high blood pressure, and morbid obesity. Also, place someone in charge of your finances. Make sure that you pay your bills and leave enough money for your commissary needs and phone expenses once you start your federal sentence. Make sure you are not late in reporting to your designation.

HINT

Bring a nice pair of sneakers and a good casual watch. They may allow you to keep these when you enter the facility. Write down a list of phone numbers, addresses and emails that you want to have access to and mail them to yourself the day before you self surrender. You may have pending legal work or appeals in process, and you are allowed to bring these documents with you.

Bail

After the arraignment, the Judge decides to grant you bail. Bail is a privilege that should not be wasted. There are certain conditions that you must adhere to while on bail. You will have to meet once a month or bi-weekly with a probation officer. You may have to document certain movements to and/or from work. You may have to be drug tested, or have travel restrictions. You should be relieved that you are granted bail, but now you must focus on "the task at hand". First, you must secure the best legal eagle available within your budget. The lawyer must evaluate all of the evidence against you and decide if you have a chance at trial. If not, he must concentrate all of his efforts to negotiate the best deal for you.

Plea Agreement

A plea agreement is basically a deal brokered between your lawyer and the government. You admit that you were engaged in criminal activity, have seen the error of your ways, and accept responsibility for your actions. In return, the prosecutor will set lower sentencing recommendations for your acceptance. This saves the government time and money by not going to trial. Almost 95% of federal cases are solved via plea bargains. People are afraid to fight the government because they are strong and powerful and will manipulate the truth to ensure you are found guilty. If you do go to trial, in many cases you will double or triple the sentence you could have served by accepting the final plea agreement offer.

Trial

Going to trial is a constitutional right we have as citizens of the United States. It is believed that we are innocent until proven guilty.

Remember, that philosophy was developed in the 1700 and 1800s. Now we are treated as guilty until proven innocent. When going to trial, remember that you will be looking at substantially more time if you blow trial. Also, it is extremely expensive to go to trial. You will have to bear the legal costs of an attorney who bills hourly and any expense you may have to incur to present or confirm your specific point of view. However, at certain times, trial proceedings are necessary because there is no plea deal on the table and the charges now against you would warrant considerable incarceration time, if not life. These are choices you must make with the proper legal eagles concerning the details of your case.

PSR/PSI Report – Pre-Sentence Report

This report is ordered by the District Judge after accepting your guilty plea or after your trial when a jury of your peers finds you guilty of the charged crimes against you. A probation officer will be assigned to your case. Have your lawyer present at all times. The PSR will give the judge the power to either lower your sentence if you have mitigating circumstances or increase your sentence if you have always been a bad or vindictive person. The report gives the judge a history of your life. It highlights the ups and downs. It will include your work, family and educational histories. It will document any physical ailments you have or chronic health conditions. It will illustrate and analyze any abusive substance use or behavior. The probation office should be informed if your judgment on the street was impaired by alcohol or drug addiction. If so, the judge can recommend the RDAP Program for you if drugs played a role in your criminal behavior. This program is an intensive 9 month program which can help you battle your drug or alcohol addiction and allow you to receive up to an additional 12 months of good time upon completion. It will help you get into the RDAP Program if your substance abuse is included in your PSR and recommended by the judge. Finally, the PSR reviews the charges you are guilty of and takes into account any historical mitigating circumstances. Then, the PSR recommends a sentencing range for the judge to review and decide upon. Also, the government would outline if you cooperated with the government on your case or provided leads of other felonies being committed in their jurisdictions. A "5K" letter will also reduce your time and will be attached to your PSR.

Sentencing Procedures

Okay, the game is finally over. It's time to face the consequences of our actions. Your lawyer files a sentencing memorandum for the judge. It recommends to the judge what would be the least amount of time necessary for the defendant to serve and correct his aberrant behavior. During this time, the judge will allow your lawyer and the prosecutor to explain the factors concerning why you should be given a lenient or harsh sentence. Your lawyer should also present any requests concerning any medical issues you may have. Also, it would be good at this time to request that the judge recommend federal prison facilities that are close to your home or considered "sweet" places to do your time. After the judge considers all the factors concerning the sentencing phase, he will "on the record" dole out your punishment. If you are on bail, you can request to self-surrender at the facility you are designated to, (see Self-Surrender). If you were in custody during pre-trial status, chances are they will return you back to the Federal Detention Center or county jail until your federal designation is decided.

CHAPTER 2

What Type of Facility Will I Be Designated To

After you are sentenced, the Bureau of Prison's Grand Prairie, Texas office will review your PSR and designate you to a prison. They will consider a lot of different factors in calculating your security and custody levels. Did your crime contain violence? Are you a member of organized crime or a gangbanger? Are you a first time offender or a career criminal? Are you a sexual predator? After evaluating you they will arrive at a custody and security score. There are five levels of incarceration, which we will explain shortly. Security levels are adhered to first. For example, you might have committed a non-violent white collar crime. However, you were sentenced to 24 years. You will have to go to a medium facility because your sentence is over 20 years, which exceeds the ceiling for being placed in a FCI Low Facility. Your risk of flight is higher because of your long sentence.

The Five Types of Correctional Facilities

Federal Prison Camp

A federal prison camp is a minimal security facility. Camps are what the public refers to as "Club Fed". They are similar to summer camps or a college campus. Campers have low custody scores between 0 – 11 points and must have no more than 10 years remaining on their sentence. In most cases, there are no fences around these prisons. If desired, any inmate could simply walk off the compound and re-enter society. Of course, if they do not return within 72 hours they would be charged with escape and have to serve up to another 5 years in addition to what they already are serving. If they do return within 72 hours, they would be given a disciplinary shot and transferred to a low facility. Some inmates go straight to a camp but may have initially started at a low or a medium facility. Violence is very minimal because the inmate security level is out-custody or community custody and the time is sweet compared to living in a low or a medium facility. Sexual predators or "chomos" are excluded from going to a camp. Under no circumstances can they enter a federal community camp before their sentence is completed. All sexual predators that have completed their sentence must adhere to strict sexual offender registers. They must alert the community they are returning to and register their sexual offender status. They are excluded from parks, fast food places, playgrounds, schools, and other areas where kids congregate and could be put at risk by the deviant behavior. Also, illegal aliens are not allowed to go to a camp for obvious flight risks. If allowed to go to a camp, they would try to run and avoid deportation back to their country. So remember, camps are great. There are a lot of privileges and you are separated from a lot of garbage that resides in the lows or mediums. Violence is minimal and you should strive to go to a camp by programming and exhibiting good behavior. We will touch upon these subjects in later chapters.

Remember, to be eligible for a camp, your custody points must be between 0 – 11, and your remaining time to serve on your sentence must not exceed 10 years.

FCI Low Facility

An FCI Low is the next type of federal facility you can be housed in. The FCI Lows contain a large, diverse pool of inmates who are serving between 1 – 20 years for a variety of different crimes. In a Low, your custody points must be between 12 and 15; with no more than 20 years remaining on your sentence. They also are the largest number of facilities in the Federal system. They contain the largest inmate pool; hence, they are the most overcrowded. FCI Lows are fenced facilities. The custody level is still very secure. You have deportable aliens, drug dealers, sexual offenders, murderers, and white collar criminals. You have Italian and Russian mobsters and a lot of gangs. There are the Bloods, Crips, Latin Kings, and every other ethnic group.

You may have non-violent crime and low custody points. However, you were sent to a Low because you are serving 20 years. You can still get to a camp. Each year they review your file and if you show them you have been programming and maintaining good behavior, they will reduce 1 – 2 points off your custody score. Also, if you receive your GED or get an outstanding job performance report, that always looks good. Violence has somewhat increased at this level because of the high influx of pedophiles that are being sent there. These inmates have developed a great hate by all other inmates. Even with all the racial tension at the Low, all inmates of every race try in a joint effort to abuse and torture pedophiles. At FCI Fort Dix, one pedophile was thrown down the stairs and died when he broke his neck. Other incidents when we were there included extortion, random beatings in the middle of the night, and property robberies when they left the room. "Chomos" must keep a low profile. If they mind their business and stay out of the way, other inmates may allow them some level of comfort there. If they find out that the pedophile sexually assaulted some young kids they will never be safe and may have to spend their entire sentence in solitary confinement in the Special Housing Unit. FCI Lows are also considered to be somewhat sweeter than the Mediums and USPs, but the level of violence at Lows has accelerated from prior periods of incarceration.

FCI Mediums

Now we are getting to the big boys. Mediums contain a large, diverse population as well as a complete array of charges. To qualify for medium status, your custody points have to be higher than 15 but less than 20 points. Medium facilities are okay if you are not a sexual offender, "chomo", or cooperated with the Government. If you are, life will be difficult here. Your security time includes sentences up to life. Obviously, at this level the crime you committed most likely contained violence, implied threats, or murder. The security level at the facilities is rated higher and they consider these inmates more deadly and dangerous. You have inmates doing 20 or 30 years, if not doing life. They do not put up with bullshit and respect is expected here. If you are out of line, a severe beating or death might be appropriate for you. The inmates are housed in mandatory 2 man cells which are locked between 8:30 and 9:00 pm each night, and reopened after the 5:00 am count for breakfast the next morning. They lock them up like animals to ensure safety throughout the evening. If you have a problem with your cellie, violence can pop-off at any time and a slow response time and lack of mobility will result in a severe beating if not death. They do not tolerate stealing or snitching. If you do either, your life is in immediate danger and you will have to enter protective custody. Inmates prepare for war by making knives and other weapons should the need arise. You should know there are metal detectors everywhere and frequent shakedowns for weapons or contraband.

Contraband includes drugs, cigarettes, liquor, or other outside comfort items. In Mediums, there is a strict protocol followed. Inmates hang out with other inmates of the same race. For example, white people hang with white guys, black with black, Spanish with Spanish, and Italian with Italian. Now you are not precluded from hanging out with only your kind. There is obvious business that transpires between the races and friendships do cross some lines. However, when you enter a facility, you have to find out where you belong. A good friend of mine was in a Medium facility and he was Italian, so when he arrived at Otisville, a Medium, he was scooped up by the Italians. They check out your paperwork first and make sure you are not a pedophile or a rat. Then they accept you and help you out with hygiene items or food until you go to commissary. They also provide important information about the facility and other inmates. At Mediums and USPs, inmates are segregated by race. They won't put a black guy and a white guy together. Now remember, if your paperwork is good, you can do a great bid at a Medium. The respect level is so much higher and the quality of inmate is better even though more dangerous. Also, you can work your way down to a low facility by lowering your custody and security. To qualify as Medium status, your points must be between 16 -23 points with no restriction on the amount you have to serve.

United States Penitentiary or Federal Penitentiary

Now you are with the serious big boys. This is the next highest level in the Federal system. Here there are many inmates serving life for dangerous and violent crimes. You rarely see any white-collar criminals here. The most dangerous people in the world are contained here. The facility is fenced in, electrified, and there is usually and 25 – 40 foot wall after the fences to contend with. Also, there are towers around the facility that contain guards with "shoot to kill" orders if an inmate is trying to escape. The respect level is the highest here and the races tend to really cling to their own. Rats or pedophiles cannot live here peacefully. There are many killings each year in the USPs. Fights over money, disrespect, or improper jail etiquette could land you in a body bag. Movements here are restricted and controlled. Correctional Officers treat you with much more respect and don't sweat the little things. Once again, you can work your way down to a medium if your custody points and security level are lowered by programming and keeping your behind out of danger's way.

Super-Max, Florence, Colorado

If you are designated here, that usually means that society has labeled you a monster and so dangerous that you will never see the streets again. This group includes serial killers, sexual deviants, terrorists, and mobsters. These people are in solitary confinement for 23 hours per day. They are allowed one hour of recreation per day, if available. The TVs, phones, and showers are usually contained within their cells to minimize movement outside of the cells. Any movement within these cells is tightly monitored. You enter a Super-Max by foot and leave in a body bag. All sentences are life. There is not much to comment on with this subject because we believe no one we are dealing with would reach this notoriety.

SHU (Special Housing Unit)

The Special Housing Unit is not a good place to land in. You are locked up in a cell for disciplinary reasons or investigation by SIS for some prohibited acts you are accused of doing. You do not have your property and if you are lucky, they may give you a radio. You can also be put into a facility's SHU if they did not have time to evaluate your file or no beds were available because of overcrowding. You may also be waiting to transfer if your points went up because of a fight or disciplinary shot. We will touch on disciplinary shots and transfers later in the book. Also, if your life is threatened or your safety is in question, you could be placed in protective custody. You can request it yourself if you get into a situation or a problem arises that you cannot contain.

HINTS

You have to make the best of it. You will be designated and sent to a facility that fits your needs based on the scoring of a Federal office worker in Grand Prairie, Texas. We recommend that you have your paperwork available. You don't need your PSR if you have a current J & C. The J & C will list all charges in your criminal judgment and indicate if you cooperated with the government and received a downward departure. The J & C will give you the time each count carries and the cumulative amount of time you must serve. When you arrive at prison, people will try and find you. They will welcome you with open arms if you pass the muster test (rat or pedophile). Also, they will see how you conduct yourself in their environment. Please keep your circle of friends small. The more people you associate with, the more potential problems you will encounter. Do not hang out or talk to people who are not cleared and labeled good. If you hang out with pedophiles or rats, people will classify you as one and treat you accordingly. Do not disrespect others by being noisy, cutting lines, or talking about matters that are not your business. Do not talk to or become friends with gay people. Do not gamble or accumulate debts for things you can't afford. Sometimes people run up gambling or drug bills and can't pay. This is not good and could lead to a serious problem and your people may not stand behind you. There are store guys who sell you food now at a higher price, and when your time comes to go to the store, they will give you a list to replace those items plus interest. Unless you have a steady cash flow from the street, don't accumulate debts with time constraints. Debts equal problems, problems, and more problems. To complete your time in a less stressful environment, stay tight, mind your own business, and respect others. It's always better to prevent the problem by steering clear of it, then by getting into a problem and trying to climb out.

CHAPTER 3

Your Home Jail

Okay, you have been designated to your prison today. When your bus arrives at your destination you and the other inmates on that bus will be brought into that facility's R & D area. The R & D area is the intake for receiving and departing inmates. You will be placed in various bullpens (cells) until the staff arrives and begins processing each of you individually. The first thing they will do is have you fill out paperwork. The first form they give you is your written consent to allow the facility to receive mail and other correspondence from the street. They let you know that all incoming mail is received and opened by the mail room before it's delivered to you. The second form requires your written permission for the Government to open and deposit financial instruments and money transfers for deposits on your behalf. These monies will be accepted and cleared by normal channels and then credited to your commissary account. This enables you to go to commissary and put money on your phone account and make telephone calls. The third form allows the facility to open a phone account for your use. They inform you the phone calls are monitored by the correctional officers of that facility. The phone area screens all calls to make sure that inmates are not doing anything illegal or threatening anyone on the streets. After incarceration, it is illegal to engage in any business activity whether legitimate or not. Another form concerns your mental health. Psychology Services wants an overview of your mental health state upon entering prison.

Have you been sexually abused? Are you on narcotics and have you developed chemical dependencies on prescribed or illegal narcotics? Are you having suicidal thoughts at this time? Would you like to see a mental health specialist at this time? Are you suffering from anxiety or depression? Yet another form is the facilities medical department. They ask you to list all physical ailments and chronic care conditions. They ask you what medications you are presently taking. Do you need a wheelchair, cane, or walker? Do you have sleep apnea and did you arrive with a CPAP machine? The medical department is thorough and will make sure they give you a week to ten days supply of drugs until they can schedule a formal appointment with a doctor for your initial exam.

A representative from Laundry will be there to strip search you and give you clean clothes for the day. The next day, early in the morning (6:00 to 6:30 am), the Laundry department will be open to fit all of the arriving inmates. Get there early so you can contend with your clothes without being rushed. Here they will issue you multiple sets of underwear, pants, shirts, socks, coats, towels, and boots. We will cover Laundry's responsibilities in later chapters. Also, on the first day you will receive a bunk roll. A bunk roll includes the blanket, sheets, and pillow for your bed. Remember, your bed must be made military style no later than 7:30 am each morning, Monday through Friday.

You will also be fingerprinted, and have to give a sample of DNA, and given your personal ID card. You must carry this ID on you at all times. You need your ID to go to the commissary and will have to scan it at every meal in the chow hall. Take care of your ID, put it in a wallet or buy an ID card protector at the commissary. You also need to present your ID when you have callouts, medical or to pick up legal mail.

You will also see a counselor from the compound that has to initially clear you to enter population. They will ask you if you testified against anyone or assisted any law enforcement agency. You must be truthful because if you did cooperate against someone, a danger may exist if either they or their co-defendants are on the compound.

After all of you have been processed you will either be going to your final unit or a special Admissions and Orientation (A & O) building. For example, at Fort Dix you are temporarily house in an A & O building until you have finished your admission and orientation. You are then assigned to your unit where you will be housed. At other prisons, you go straight to your housing unit and have to attend A & O classes. A & O classes must be attended by each inmate. During these classes, they will inform you of that facility's daily activities and what they expect from you during your stay.

Let's say that you are going into population after R & D has finished processing your group. The first thing you do is take all of your belongings to the unit you are assigned to. A CO will be waiting for your arrival and will show you where your living quarters are. Go to your room or cell and start making up your bed. Upon entering the building, you will see how your bunk and living quarters are to be maintained. Look for your people to welcome. Introduce yourself to your roommates. You will notice your people will come to you. They will ask you where you are from and based on race or location; take you to the right people. Prisons are segregated in two ways. The first is by race, and the next is by location. Guys strengthen their friendships via the racial or location card. For example, you may be black and I may be white, and we are both from New York. In prison, they have cars – which mean a group of fellows bonded by prior living locations, not necessarily by race. We can have a New York car that consists of men from every race or religion. It's important to join a car or racial group in prison. These will become your friends and homies during the good times and the bad times of your incarceration.

If you are not a pedophile or rat, you can go to your group's Shotcaller if you have a problem that needs to be resolved. A Shotcaller is a group's number one ranked man. He is the decision maker and problem solver for his people. Each group has a Shotcaller to help mediate problems before they escalate into a flat-out war that results in stabbings, lock-downs, and transfers.

Inmate ID Registration Number

Your inmate ID is very important. You must have it on you whenever you are leaving the unit. You especially need your ID card when you have medical callouts and for chow. The medical services area will not attempt to initiate any medical treatment without confirming your identity. Your ID registration number is composed of two components. My ID for example, states my full name and register number. My register is ****2-054. The number ****2 represents my individual federal number, and 054 represents the Second District which is located in New York City. Remember, you will also need your ID card whenever you go to the dining hall. You will have to scan it before they will allow you to eat. This system prevents inmates from going in line several times when good meals (e.g. Fried Chicken) are being served. One meal per inmate, 3 time a day, 7 days a week, is the amount of food the BOP is required to serve you.

Commissary

You have a spending limit of three hundred twenty to three hundred forty dollars per month. When you spend three hundred twenty to three hundred forty dollars total, regardless of how much time is still remaining in the month, you are cut-off until you re-validate. Your re-validation date is calculated by taking the 5th digit of your Federal ID register number and multiplying it by 3 and adding 1 to it. For example, my Federal register number is ****2-054, the fifth digit is a 2, so I multiply 2 X 3 = 6 then add a 1, which equals 7. Therefore on the 7th of each month, my three hundred twenty to three hundred forty dollars spending limit in commissary reloads and becomes available. Also, you will be given 300 minutes per month to use for telephone calls. For me, on the 7th of each month, my phone re-validates back to 300 minutes.

HINT

What I like to do is budget my commissary money during the 4 weeks of the month. I usually spend one hundred twenty five to one hundred fifty dollars the first week, skip a week, and spend another seventy five to one hundred dollars the next two weeks replacing the everyday items I used (e.g. coffee, creamer, laundry powder). Remember, you have 300 minutes of phone time each month. Budget wisely and make sure you do not run out of phone minutes. In prison, anything can happen and you may transfer suddenly or become ill and need to contact your people. If you don't have minutes left, you can't do that.

CHAPTER 4

A & O and Unit Team Interactions and Functions

Admission and Orientation (A & O)

When you first arrive at your institution, you will be placed in an Admission and Orientation Program. This orientation period will consist of lectures by department heads and other staff members regarding various programs, services, policies, procedures, and regulations at that facility. You are required to attend the lectures and callouts which are part of the Admission and Orientation Program. Your attendance is mandatory; if you miss any of the lectures, you may be required to attend A & O again.

HINT

Pay attention, it is very important and informative. You can learn about the programs offered and about the various jobs that are available at the institution.

Unit Team Meeting

You are assigned to a unit team which is comprised of your Unit Manager, Case Manager, Correctional Counselor, and Education Representative. Your team members are available to assist you in many areas, including personal and family problems, counseling, parole matters, release planning and assistance in setting and attaining goals for yourself.

Program Reviews – Team

Program reviews will be held every 180 days if more than one year remains until your release date, and every 90 days if less than one year. Your educational progress, work assignments, custody status, transfer requests, Residential Re-Entry Center Placement, institutional adjustment and FRP if you have any outstanding fines or restitution will be reviewed.

Central Inmate Monitoring System

The Central Inmate Monitoring System (CIM) is a method used by the Bureau of Prisons to monitor and control the transfer, temporary release, and participation in community activities of inmates who pose special management consideration. Designation as a CIM case does not, in and of itself, prevent an inmate from participating in community or population activities. All inmates who are designated as CIM cases will be notified of their status by their case manager.

Re-designation to Another Institution

Transfer requests should be made by cop-out to the Unit Team. Ordinarily, transfer requests are considered after you have been at a facility for a minimum of 18 months with clear conduct and during your regularly scheduled review. If the Unit Team determines you have a valid reason for transfer, a recommendation will be made to the Designations and Sentence Computation Center for a final decision. Additionally, a transfer to a place closer to your release residence will be considered if you are 500 miles or greater from your release residence.

Parole Application

If you are eligible for parole, it is necessary that you file a written application using the approved parole application form. Your case manager will assist you in this regard and schedule your hearing.

Transfer to Foreign Countries/Treaty Transfer

The BOP is authorized to transfer custody of a foreign citizen who is serving a sentence in the United States to his country of citizenship for completion of his sentence. Such a transfer is voluntary and is subject to the approval of both countries. Those individuals with committed fines may not be transferred without the permission of the U.S. District Court which imposed the fine. Your case manager will provide additional information regarding transfer procedures.

Release Preparation Program

Each inmate is expected to participate in all categories of the Release Preparation Program. Inmates who refuse to participate should be aware that their refusal may affect eligibility or length of participation in community-based programs (i.e. furloughs, Re-Entry Centers). When you are within two years of release, you may become involved in a program in which members of the community are involved. This includes Community Correction Managers, U.S. Probation Services, and staff members from halfway houses who will provide release information to you when visiting the institution.

Residential Re-Entry Center

The purpose of the Residential Re-Entry Center is to enable you to experience a transition period between incarceration and release. Every inmate does not qualify for release through a halfway house and eligibility will be determined on an individual basis by the unit team. The recommended length of stay in a halfway house will also be a unit team decision.

Detainers

Warrants based on pending charges, overlapping consecutive, or unsatisfied sentences in Federal, State, or military jurisdictions will be accepted as detainers. You should make every effort to resolve any pending charges originating from the above sources. The Interstate Agreement on Detainers is the method to resolve detainers. An actual detainer must be on file in order for you to file for a resolution of the detainer under the Interstate Agreement or Detainers.

Furloughs

A furlough is an authorized absence from an institution by an inmate who is not under escort of a staff member or a U.S. Marshal. A furlough is not a right, but a privilege granted an inmate who meets certain requirements. You must have community custody, maintain above average work, clean quarters and sanitation reports and have a high school diploma or GED. You must also be medically cleared, have not used drugs or alcohol during the past two years and maintained a minimum of six months clear conduct. Additionally, you must have demonstrated significant financial responsibility and a furlough must not depreciate the seriousness of your offense or create public concern. Contact your unit staff for additional furlough information.

CHAPTER 5

Administration/Unit Staff – All Federal Facilities

Warden

The warden is the Federal authority on all matters within the facility. His/her decisions are based upon policies established by the Bureau of Prisons. While he/she is responsible for the total operation of the institution, he/she has delegated certain duties and responsibilities to the other staff.

Unit Manager

The unit manager implements decisions made the by Warden that pertain to programs and the daily operation of the facility. If you have a problem you believe has not been resolved, after exhausting all other avenues, an inmate Request to Staff form should be submitted to the unit manager.

Case Manager

The case manager is responsible for all case work services and prepares classification material, progress reports, release plans, correspondence, and other materials related to your confinement. The case manager serves as a liaison between the inmate, the administration, and the community. The case manager is a member of the Unit Disciplinary Committee.

Counselor

The counselor provides counseling and guidance regarding areas pertaining to institutional adjustment and personal difficulties. They participate in the development of meaningful programs. The counselor will visit inmate work assignments regularly. They should be consulted regarding problems you encounter during your incarceration. They ordinarily perform functions concerning administrative complaints, visitors list, financial responsibility issues, mail, telephone lists and property.

Secretary

The secretary is responsible for all clerical functions and a significant portion of the administrative duties necessary for the facility's operation.

Classification Team

The classification team ordinarily includes the unit manager, case manager, counselor, and education advisor. The unit officer will provide the team with a summary of your adjustment within the housing unit including sanitation, interaction with staff and inmates, and any other information which may be relevant. Generally, the resolution of matters or interests while at this institution is most appropriately initiated with the Unit Team. Matters such as custody, transfers, security level, residential re-entry center placement, etc. are discussed during your regularly scheduled team meeting which occur every 6 months. When you have under a year to serve, these team meetings are every 3 months.

Unit Disciplinary Committee

The rules and regulations of your facility are enforced to provide an orderly, safe environment for all inmates. The Unit Disciplinary

Committee is comprised of your unit staff. All incident reports (shots) are processed through the Unit Disciplinary Committee within 3 days of an alleged incident. Incident reports written for serious or repetitive violations may be sent to the Disciplinary Hearing Officer (DHO) for disposition.

Extra Duty

There is an option the Correctional Officer of your unit or other staff members can give you instead of a disciplinary shot when you are caught doing a prohibited act. Extra duty might include mowing the lawn, cleaning an area of the unit or cleaning the compound. At Fort Dix, I got caught smoking, so instead of writing a shot and having a written incident report in my jacket, I mowed the softball field. They try to embarrass you in front of your friends and sometimes they need extra help. Always try to convince the CO or officer who caught you to give you extra duty. If he writes a shot, it usually will stick. You can lose your commissary, phone, visiting and/or email privileges. Also, the shot is assigned points based on the severity level. If the shot increases your points, you may have to transfer to a higher facility. It stays on your jacket for 1 year, and it will stop your camp transfer or transfer to a halfway house. So remember, should you get caught, beg for extra duty. Also, never rat out other people in an effort to save your ass. Jailhouse snitches are usually dealt with in a just fashion. If you can't live with the consequences of being caught doing a prohibited act, then don't do it.

Management Variable

Unit Staff can place a management variable on you which can override your custody level. For example, you are a problem individual or at risk of flight based on your circumstances. Now let's say your points are 7, which qualifies you for a camp. If the Unit Team thinks that it is not beneficial to send you to a camp, which is out custody, they can place a "Greater Security, Close Supervision" management variable on you. This will prohibit you from being able to go to a camp. Management variables are time-based and do expire if your behavior and conduct remains clear. For example, my friend's points in 2006 were 3 points; he was a clerk in Education at Fort Dix. One day, they sent him and his friend Dale to the Philadelphia SHU for an Office of Inspector General investigation. They were trying to prove that he and Dale were given preferential treatment from the staff. They said the staff was bringing them cigarettes, food from the street, and allowed us to make unmonitored phone calls from their offices. After 6 months in Philly, there was not proof of foul play, however, the BOP placed a management variable on him for two years. This prohibited him from being able to transfer to a camp. They also sent him on "diesel therapy"; he traveled to 3 prisons, all Lows.

Disciplinary Shots – Appeals Process

There is an appeals process when you receive a "shot" for any prohibited act. You will be given an opportunity to dispute the shot. When you first are given a shot, you go to the Lieutenant's office and he reads it to you. He listens to what you have to say. If he thinks it is a weak or a petty shot, he can squash it right there. If it is a valid shot, he will send it to UDC or DHO to finalize it and sanction you. For first time or petty shots, they can decide to suspend your penalty and put it on the shelf. If you maintain clear conduct for a period of time, usually 3 months to a year, the shot perishes and stays off your jacket. However, if you get in any more trouble during this time period, they will reinstate the suspended shot plus give you a new shot. To appeal the shot you have to wait until UDC or DHO finds you guilty of that act. Usually, on the bottom of the disciplinary report they give you instructions on how to state your case and mail it to the appropriate office for review. Your sanctions are in effect until you win your appeal. Should you lose your appeal, they can increase your sanction for trying to beat it.

HINT

When you get a shot you will be called to the Lieutenant's office. Ask them to give you extra duty. Show remorse for your actions and tell them you won't get in any more trouble. Remember, if a shot sticks to your jacket it could hurt you in trying to transfer to a lower security facility and/or halfway house. Blood, sweat, and tears are better than a black and white notation documenting a disciplinary problem.

List of the Disciplinary Shots and Their Respective Levels of Severity

Series 100 Shots – Greatest Severity Level

- Killing
- Assaulting any Person
- Escape
- Setting a Fire
- Possession of a Weapon
- Rioting
- Encouraging Others to Riot
- Taking Hostages
- Possession of Hazardous Tools

- Refusing to Take a Urine Test or Breathalyzer

- Introduction of Narcotics, Alcohol, etc.

- Use of Narcotics, alcohol, etc.

- Sexual Assault

- Destroying/Disposing of an Item During Search

- Use of Mail for the Purpose of Committing Another Severe Act

- Use of the Telephone for the Purpose of Committing Another Severe Act

- Interfering with a Staff Member in the Performance of their Duties

- Conduct which Interferes with the Security of, or Orderly Running of the Institution or BOP

Series 200 Shots – High Severity Level

- Escape from a work detail or non-secure institution

- Fighting

- Threatening bodily harm

- Extortion/blackmail

- Engaging in sexual acts

- Making sexual proposals

- Wearing a disguise or mask

- Possession of an authorized locking device

- Adulteration of any food or drink

- Possession of officer/staff clothing

- Engaging in a group demonstration

- Encouraging others to refuse to work

- Giving or offering a bribe to staff or officer
- Giving money for contraband
- Destroying Government property
- Stealing
- Demonstrating martial arts or boxing
- Being in an unauthorized area with a person of the opposite sex
- Assaulting any person – injuries limited
- Stalking
- Possession of stolen property
- Refusing a required physical test or examination
- Tattooing or self-mutilation "Domino in the penis trick"
- Sexual assault – "getting head from a fag"
- Use of telephone for illegal purposes
- Use of mail for illegal purposes
- Interfering with staff
- Disruptive conduct that interferes with security
- Series 300 Shot – Moderate Severity Level
- Indecent exposure
- Misuse of medication
- Possession of money
- Loaning property for profit
- Possession of anything unauthorized
- Refusing to work
- Refusing to obey staff order
- Violating a furlough

- Violating a halfway house
- Unexcused absence from work or program
- Failing to perform work instructed by officer
- Insolence/talking bad to a staff member
- Lying to staff/CO
- Counterfeiting documents/forms
- Participating in an unauthorized gathering
- Being in an unauthorized area
- Failure to follow safety/sanitation regulations
- Using equipment/machinery without authorization
- Failure to stand for count
- Interfering with count
- Gambling
- Preparing a gambling pool
- Possession of gambling paraphernalia
- Unauthorized contact with public
- Giving money/property to another inmate without staff authorization
- Destroying government property valued below one hundred dollars.
- Being unsanitary/untidy
- Possession of non-hazardous tools
- Smoking
- Fraudulent/Deceptive testing (e.g. GED cheating)
- Conducting a business

- Gang activity/communication
- Circulating a petition
- Use of mail for criminal activity
- Use of telephone for criminal activity
- Interfering with staff duties
- Interfering with security or institutional conduct

Penalties for Series 100 – 300

- Recommend parole date rescission or retardation
- Forfeit or withhold earning statutory good time or non-vested good conduct time (up to 100%) and terminate or disallow extra good time (Disallow is ordinarily between 50% and 75% (27-41 days) of good conduct time credit available for a year
- Disciplinary segregation (up to 12 months)
- Monetary restitution
- Monetary fine
- Loss of privileges (i.e. visitation, telephone, commissary, recreation, movies)
- Change housing quarters
- Removal from program/activity
- Loss of job
- Recommend transfer to another facility
- Additional criminal charges
- Impound property
- Extra duty

Series 400 – Low Severity Level

- Malingering, feigning illness
- Using abusive or obscene language
- Conduct with a visitor in violation of BOP regulations
- Unauthorized physical contact (kissing, hugging)
- Interfering with a staff member's duties
- Interfering with the security of the institution

Penalties for Series 400 Level

- Disallow ordinarily up to 12.5% (1-7 days) of good conduct time credit available for year. Disallow ordinarily up to 25% (1-14 days) of good conduct time available for year (if found to have committed 3rd violation of the same prohibited act)
- Monetary restitution
- Monetary fine
- Loss of privileges (i.e. visitation, telephone, commissary, movies, recreation)
- Change housing quarters
- Removal from program/group activity
- Loss of job
- Impound property
- Confiscate Contraband
- Restrict to quarters
- Extra duty

CHAPTER 6

Count Times

The purpose of a count is to ensure all inmates are accounted for at the institution. The officers conducting the count must be able to see living, breathing inmates. When this is not accomplished, especially during the morning watch count times, the officer will wake you up to ensure accountability of each inmate. Count times will be announced over the public address system.

Weekdays	
Weekends/Holidays	12 am
No Standing Count	12 am
No Standing Count	3 am
No Standing Count	3 am
No Standing Count	5 am
No Standing Count	5 am
No Standing Count	4 pm
Stand Up Count	10 am
Stand Up Count	10 pm
Stand Up Count	4 pm
Stand Up Count	10 pm
Stand Up Count	

There are also special times when count is called (e.g. Fog Count, Fight Occurs, Escapes, etc.).

Every month they do a lock-down census, either in the morning or afternoon. You must be at work, education, or have a medical callout.

If you are not where you belong, you can get an incident report. We will touch on this in a later chapter.

HINTS

Always be by your bunk at the designated times. Even if they are running late you don't ever want to be absent when they are counting your room, dormitory, cubicle, or cell. COs get very angry when you mess up their count, they can retaliate by giving you a shot, locking you up in the SHU, giving you extra duty, or by shaking down you and your roommate's personal property. This leads to trouble, trouble, and more trouble. Be prompt and orderly; no talking during the count. Count does not take a lot of time. You can wait until they clear count before you dive into something to do.

Callouts

The callout sheet is a schedule of appointments for that day. This includes medical, dental, educational, team meetings and other activities. It is posted on the unit bulletin boards by 4:00 pm on the day preceding the appointment. It is your responsibility to check the callout sheet for appointments daily and to attend all scheduled appointments. You must bring your ID. Failure to report to callouts will result in disciplinary action. Also, it is important to always report to callouts in case there is a census count. You have to be in full uniform.

HINT

Always be where you are supposed to be at the time you are supposed to be there and you will have smooth sailing. If not, you will catch an out-of-bounds shot.

Cop-Outs

Use these forms to request something from staff. It is a formal inmate request to staff form. Staff must reply to all cop-outs within 24 - 36 hours. Always keep a copy of your cop-out. You can get a cop-out form from your counselor and they have blank forms in the library.

Cop-Outs Are Used For
- Requesting medical information or help
- Requesting a job
- Requesting an educational or vocational class
- Room changes
- Vacation time
- Requesting an attorney unmonitored call
- Special visit from your family

HINT

Always keep blank cop-out forms on hand.

Work

Everyone will have a work assignment after you are medically cleared. Your first work assignment will be based on institutional needs, available jobs, your past work experience, and evaluation of your skills. Any job preference should be indicated during your interview with Unit Staff.

Work Assignment

When you have worked on a job for a period of 90 days and desire a job change, you should prepare an Inmate Request to Staff (cop-out) indicating what job you want and a detailed reason for the change. Your current work supervisor and the supervisor of the requested work assignment must both be indicated in writing, and both in agreement of the change of jobs. Your request will then be considered by your Unit Team. You will be notified if a work reassignment is warranted and your name will appear on the institution change sheets, which are posted daily on the inmate bulletin boards.

Work and Institutional Rules

Whether you are assigned to an inside or outside detail, you must stay on your work assignment at all times. If you have a valid reason for leaving your work site (call-out), you must notify your work supervisor and obtain authorization. If you are injured while performing your assigned duties, you must immediately report this injury to your work supervisor. You must use proper and specified precautions such as steel-toed shoes, goggles, gloves, and safety devices which are supplied for your protection. No radios, reading material, food items, or personal clothing are permitted on the work site.

UNICOR

To be placed on the UNICOR waiting list a signed request to a staff member must be submitted.

Working Hours

Ordinarily working hours are from 7:30 am until 3:45 pm, Monday through Friday. Each work day provides for a lunch break.

Idle, Convalescence, and Medical Assignments

When it is necessary to restrict the inmate's activities due to health concerns, an inmate may be placed on Idle, Convalescence or Medically Unassigned status. The medical staff will issue you a Medical Duty Status Form that identifies your limitations. It is the inmate's responsibility to deliver one copy to his work supervisor and one copy to his unit officer. The following is a synopsis of restrictions for each type of medical limitation status:

Idle – temporary disability not to exceed three days duration including weekends and holidays. You will be restricted to your room except for meals, barbering, religious services, sick call, visits, and call-outs. No recreational activity.

Convalescence – Recovery period for an operation, injury, or serious illness. Not less than 4 days and not to exceed 30 days, subject to renewal. You are excused from work and may not participate in recreational activities.

Medically Unassigned/Disabled – in the event of a serious medical problem or a medical disability that would require a protracted period of convalescence you will be removed from your work detail assignment and placed on medically unassigned status. You will remain on total sports restriction. You may leave your unit for meals, medication, visits, regularly scheduled religious services, call-outs, and medical appointments.

HINT

Do not get caught performing unauthorized activities when you are medically unassigned. They will remove you from this status immediately and remove all benefits you may have enjoyed while in this status.

Restricted Duty

Restricted from specific activities because of existing physical or mental handicap for a specific time period, or indefinitely.

Food Services

The only medical restrictions from being assigned to Food Services are chronic infectious diarrhea, chronic draining lesion, and Hepatitis B or C.

Additional Tips

When choosing a job, you must decide if you really want to make money or just work the absolute minimal to get by. If you want to make a lot of money, I would suggest that you sign up for UNICOR. UNICOR is a prison company that pays the best hourly wages. You can move up to a grade 1 or 2 and earn between one hundred fifty and two hundred dollars per month. There is also overtime available and bonuses if you meet quotas or have longevity status. The average paying job is fifteen to twenty five dollars, so you see that UNICOR offers a lot of opportunity. However, UNICOR is strict, no goofing off -- unexplained absences and poor working habits will lead to your dismissal. Commissary is another high paying job. You can earn between one hundred twenty five and one hundred seventy five dollars per month. You will have to lift heavy pallets when stacking the food shelves and remain on your feet to process all of the daily commissary orders.

Food Service Hustle

People in food service eat well and can make a lot of money selling extra food during the meal and later on in the individual units. People crave chicken, roast beef, eggs, bread, and vegetables. They also sell cooking oil, pasta, spices, special cakes, chicken patties, and burgers.

After a meal is served the leftovers are given to the workers to either eat or sell back in the units. You have to be careful, if you get caught leaving the kitchen with large amounts of food, you can get a shot. However, if you work hard and are on good terms with that CO, he will usually look the other way. But remember, if you get caught later in the unit, don't rat on your CO. Good kitchen workers can make two hundred fifty and four hundred dollars per month depending how hard they work. The guys who make the most usually are hard-working inmates who have been there awhile and know the ins and outs of that facility's kitchen environment.

Unit Orderlies

These people are assigned to clean the unit and keep it in tip-top shape. Many people are assigned a specific area to clean. They can choose to clean it or hire someone to do it for them. There are a lot of no-show jobs, such as unit orderly. Hook-up with your unit's head orderly and let him know you want a no-show job. Usually, you just hand over the pay to the person doing your job. No job allows you to work out more, do your legal work, or relax.

Fines and Restitution – Financial Responsibility Program

All designated inmates are required to develop a plan to meet financial obligations. These include special assessments, court ordered restitution, fines, court costs, judgments in favor of the United States, other debts owed the Federal government, and other court ordered obligations (e.g. child support, alimony, etc.). Your unit team will assist you in developing a financial plan to satisfy your obligations, but you are responsible for making all payments either from your earnings with the institution or from outside sources. Ordinarily, the minimum payment for non-UNICOR inmates will be twenty five to fifty dollars per quarter. UNICOR workers must allot no less than 50% of their monthly pay toward their obligations. If you refuse to fulfill the financial plan developed by your unit team, you cannot work for UNICOR or receive performance pay above the maintenance level. Additionally, the status of your financial plan will be included in your progress reports, and will be considered by the unit team when determining your security/custody level, job assignment, eligibility for community activities, and preferred housing. Fine repayment schedules are also calculated by dividing a six month average of your upcoming commissary money. If you get a lot, they will expect you to pay a lot so be careful and monitor your deposits accordingly. Why give your food money to Uncle Sam when you are already giving him your time.

HINT

You may need to have money sent to your friend's account if he does not have financial obligations to meet.

CHAPTER 7

Good Time Calculation

The inmates sentenced under the Sentencing Reform Act are entitled to good time if the sentence is at least one year and one day in length. Good conduct time is based on the actual number of days served and not on the length of the sentence. The only good time available will be 54 days per year. If good conduct time is disallowed, it cannot be restored. There is a bill pending in Congress that would allow 7 extra days and bring our time down to 85% of the sentence imposed. We lose 7 days per year because good conduct time is calculated based on days served. In State prisons, good conduct time is based on the length of the sentence; i.e. 85% of 10 years is 8 ½ years, not 8 years and 7 months.

There are ways to increase your time off. A brief explanation is provided below.

Halfway House

Halfway houses are located in many U.S. cities. They allow an inmate an easier transition into society. A probation officer at the halfway house will help supervise an employment search for the inmate and help him ease back into the community and re-establish family ties. The usual rule of thumb is that you can get up to 10% off your total sentence up to 6 months. For example, as long as you are sentenced to at least 5 years (60 months) you can get up to 6 months allocated to the halfway house. Remember, a halfway house is a privilege, not a right. You need to show good behavior and programming to your Unit Team. They are responsible for putting your halfway house paperwork together and deciding how much time you deserve. On occasion, availability of beds at your

Half way house might cut into the time you receive. The Second Chance Act allows for up to one year in a halfway house for inmates who have served rather long sentences (20 plus years), have limited family ties, no place to go, and need additional supervised halfway house time to successfully re-enter society.

RDAP – Residential Drug Abuse Program

This is a program designed to rehabilitate habitual drug and alcohol offenders. The Feds put this program in several prisons at all different levels of custody. With this program you can get up to one year off and a full six months in a halfway house. It is extensive, intensive and requires a lot of work, effort and extremely good behavior. We will go into more detail about this later in this chapter.

Life Connection Program

FCI Mylan, Michigan and Petersburg, VA

This is a religious program you can apply to once you have served at least one year in prison. The federal prison chaplains at your federal correctional institution must make the recommendation. For example, my friend at Fort Dix, Pete an outlaw biker was required to go to weekly meetings for Christian religious services. After 6 to 9 months, you see the priest or chaplain of Christian Services and tell him you have an interest in this program. This program is an extensive spiritual enlightenment that takes a year to complete. Upon completion, you can apply for additional good conduct time credit up to but not exceeding one year. The program is very limited and availability of space is small because it is offered at only two Federal facilities. It's a long shot, but it has to be mentioned.

Here's how you should calculate your good conduct time. An example of 5 and 10 year sentences is illustrated:

Sentence Length = 60 months

Good Time 87.1% = times .871%

Subtotal = 52 months 8 days

Less Halfway House = 6 months

Total without RDAP = 46 months 8 days

Sentence length = 60 months

Good Time 87.1% = .871%

Subtotal = 52 months 8 days

Less RDAP = 12 months

Subtotal = 40 months 26 days

Less Halfway House = 6 months

Total with RDAP = 34 months 26 days

You can see the difference when you take RDAP. Also remember with RDAP you are guaranteed to get the full 6 months of halfway house. Let's calculate a 10 year sentence with and without utilizing the RDAP program:

Sentence Length = 120 months

Good Time 87.1% = times .871%

Subtotal = 104 months 14 days

Less Halfway House = 6 months

Total without RDAP = 98 months 14 days

Sentence Length – 120 months

Good Time 87.1% = times .871%

Subtotal = 104 months 14 days

Less RDAP = 12 months

Subtotal = 92 months 14 days

Less Halfway House = 6 months

Total = 86 months 14 days

RDAP lowers your effective sentence time down to 71.6%. That's a big difference from the stated Federal rate of 87.1%. A chart calculating good time based on your original sentence is available in the back of your book for easy reference.

Drug Education

Non-Residential Drug Treatment – 40 Hour Program:
The non-residential group is aimed at engaging motivated individuals in addressing their drug/alcohol abuse problems. These individuals are usually not yet ready, or perhaps do not meet the qualifications to participate in residential therapy. Non-residential

participants, with the drug treatment staff, develop individualized treatment plans based on an assessment of their problem and goals. Program groups will meet for 12 weeks.

Residential Drug Abuse Program – RDAP:

The RDAP provides intensive drug abuse treatment to individuals who have been diagnosed with a significant drug/alcohol use disorder. RDAP is 9 months in duration, and an additional 6 months of halfway house. Progress in treatment is based on the inmate's ability to demonstrate comprehension and internalization of treatment concepts by taking behaviorally observable action to change his unhealthy behaviors. After submitting a cop-out requesting RDAP, you will be scheduled for an interview at roughly 24 – 30 months of your remaining sentence.

RDAP Criteria:

Inmates must have a verifiable substance abuse disorder. Recreational, social or occasional use of alcohol and/or drugs that does not rise to the level of excessive or abusive drinking does not provide the required verification of a substance use disorder.

There is documentation available to verify the inmate's use of specific drugs or alcohol. Any verifying documentation of alcohol or other drug use must indicate problematic use.

Inmate must agree to adhere to the therapeutic community rules and expectations for all members.

There is sufficient time remaining on the inmate's sentence, ordinarily 24 months.

The individual has no "cognitive" impairment or learning disability that precludes participation, or is unable to participate in the program in the language in which it is conducted.

An inmate who completes the RDAP is eligible to receive up to 12 months extra good time conduct and a mandatory 6 month halfway house designation.

Early Release Ineligible

Inmates who have a prior felony or misdemeanor conviction for homicide (including death caused by recklessness, but not including death caused by negligence or justifiable homicide), forcible rape, robbery, aggravated assault, arson, kidnapping, or an offense that by its nature or conduct involves sexual abuse offenses committed upon minors.

You would automatically be ineligible if you meet any of the following criteria; inmates who have a current felony conviction for an offense that has an element, either actual or attempted, of threatened use of physical force against the person or property of another; an offense that involved the carrying, possession or use of a firearm or other dangerous weapon or explosives (including any explosive material or explosive device); an offense that by its nature or conduct presents a serious or potential risk of physical force against the person or property of another; an offense that by its nature or conduct involves sexual abuse offenses being committed upon minors. Inmates who have been convicted of attempt, conspiracy or other offenses which involved an underlying offense listed in the above paragraph, or inmates who previously received an early release under Title 18 USC 3621 (e)

HINTS

The most important thing to remember when talking to your lawyer is that you need to allow your lawyer to qualify *for RDAP. I know what you are thinking, why would I want to make myself sound worse by bringing up previous incidents of DUI, drug use, fights due to alcohol or anything else? I myself fought my own lawyer when he suggested this but by admitting to these issues I was able to participate in RDAP. The judge recommended me for the residential drug program which got me 9 months off my sentence and could have gotten me up to one full year off. Upon completion, RDAP ensures the inmate up to 12 months of extra good conduct time and 6 months at the halfway house. You must document that you had and still have a drug/alcohol problem to qualify. We can't stress this enough, even if you think you don't have a previous substance problem. You want to make sure that you let them know you have a serious drug and or alcohol problem. Remember you have to do 87% of your Federal sentence and this is one of the only chances to reduce your sentence. Also remember that they guarantee a 6 month halfway house privilege. Usually, if you don't take RDAP, your halfway house time will be geared to 10% of your sentence. For example, if you are doing 38 months and qualify for RDAP, you will get three months more of halfway house credit. You'll hit the street faster by going to RDAP. This is the only way to reduce the percentage of actual time served versus sentence received. One guy I know was given 21 years and 10 months (262 months), and with the RDAP program, he will only do approximately 196 months. His effective Federal prison time falls from 87.1% to 74.8% (196 divided by 262 months). Remember our book will pay for itself if you only learn one lesson from our advice: <u>Make Sure You Qualify for RDAP!!!</u>*

CHAPTER 8

Educational Opportunities

Education

Academic programs are directed toward assisting students in attaining basic literacy goals that will enable them to function in a world which requires a functional knowledge of reading, writing and arithmetic.

The General Educational Development Class (GED) focuses upon these important goals. Classes are offered in an assortment of educationally stimulating subjects, in addition to the basic skill areas. Educational staff is committed to practicing sound educational techniques. They are prepared to offer you the opportunity to pursue a significant course of study, leading to the attainment of functional literacy, your High School Diploma, and marketable work skills.

Law Library

The law library provides facilities for legal research and legal document preparation. For your convenience, this library is open during the daytime and most evenings. The library is provided for the benefit of the entire inmate population. The library is the designated legal photocopy site. Copies can be made using a copy card purchased from commissary.

Leisure Library

The education department maintains a leisure library. The library contains reference books, encyclopedias, college listings, and recent volumes of "Book in Print". Also available through the leisure library are numerous books which are intended to provide leisure reading for the general population. These "leisure reading" books are available to the population to be checked out for a two week period.

Fictional and non-fictional materials are available. The leisure library also contains a well-stocked Hispanic collection which provides book listings per category. The leisure library contains a wide range of magazines and periodicals. Magazines and newspapers are available in English and Spanish.

VCCLEA/PLRA

The Violent Crime Control and Law Enforcement Act (VCCLEA) applies to inmates whose offenses were on or after September 13, 1994, but before April 29, 1996. The Prison Literacy Act (PLRA) applies to inmates after April 26, 1996. Both laws require inmates who do not possess a GED or high school diploma to satisfactorily participate in the literacy program until attainment of a GED. Failure to do so may affect an inmate's good conduct time.

Academic Programs – GED – Literacy Programs

Enrollment is mandatory unless you have a documented high school diploma or GED. An inmate confined in a Federal institution who does not have a verified high school diploma is required to attend the adult literacy program. He must be enrolled for a minimum of 240 hours or until the GED is attained, whichever comes first. A high school diploma is the basic academic requirement for almost all entry level jobs. Persons who function below this level often encounter serious difficulty in obtaining employment and carrying out daily activities and responsibilities. The classes prepare the students in areas of writing skills, social studies, science, mathematics, literature, and the arts. Tutors are available for your guidance and questions. Upon completion of the GED in prison, you are rewarded with a twenty five dollar monetary bonus which is put into your commissary account. Not having your GED may hurt your pay grades and mobility for certain institutional jobs (e.g. UNICOR).

English As A Second Language (ESL)

Enrollment is mandatory for non-English speaking inmates unless you score at least an 8th grade level on the CASAS Examination.

Adult Continuing Education (ACE)

The ACE Program is designed to provide continuing educational experiences in a wide variety of subjects. Courses taught are determined by residential surveys and staff requests. Courses with a business emphasis are popular with the inmate population and help guide the future of some inmates upon release. Classes include residential real estate, managerial accounting, among others. Classes usually last 10 to 12 weeks and you will receive a certificate of completion.

Apprenticeship Training Program

The purpose of the apprenticeship program is to learn and develop a salable skill in order to gain future employment. There are several apprenticeship areas throughout an institution. These programs are offered to individuals who are interested in learning a preferred skill. At Fort Dix, they offered woodworking, picture framing, masonry, and electrical. At Lewisburg, they offer a Graphic Arts training program that leads to a marketable skill in the area of printing and graphics. Each institution has their particular area of expertise. Prospective candidates must complete a minimum of 30 to 90 days of satisfactory job performance and be recommended by the detail supervisor. A cop-out must be completed and submitted to the Apprenticeship Coordinator in order to be officially enrolled in the program. In addition to the on-the-job- training, the apprentice will receive a minimum of 15- hours of related classroom instruction from the trade instructor. These programs allow individuals the trade skills to enhance their employability chances and avoid going back to their past criminal behavior.

Parenting Program

The parenting program helps build positive relationships between inmates, their spouses, and their children during and after incarceration. The program assists inmates in identifying and counteracting negative behavior which results from a parent being incarcerated. Additionally, the program assists the inmate in his adjustment back into the community and home life.

HINTS

Education in prison is vital for a lot of inmates. By taking vocational and GED classes, they improve their intelligence and the skills necessary to obtain and keep a legitimate job. Programming is also important for your Unit Team and probation officer. They will give you more leeway and credit for trying to self-educate instead of just watching videos and playing sports while you are incarcerated. My advice - a GED is a must. Also, take ACE classes for subjects that interest you and that have good job prospects for employment upon your release. You're in prison, make the best of it, stop sulking and make positive changes now which will carry you through when you re-enter society.

CHAPTER 9

Let God Show You The Way

Religious Services

Religious Services offers a wide variety of religious programs for inmates. Chaplains of various faiths are available for pastoral care, counseling, or other professional services.

Reasons for Choosing to Speak with a Chaplain

- Difficulty adjusting to incarceration

- Personal problems, grief or loss

- Religious questions or problems

- Relationship issues with family or other inmates

- The conversation between an inmate and a Chaplain may be requested to be kept confidential, unless the conversation demonstrates that you may be a risk to yourself, another inmate, or a staff member.

Services

All regularly scheduled services, as well as special services with outside volunteers, are open to all inmates. A current copy of the religious services schedule is posted in the Chapel as well as in the housing units. Services which take place during work hours will require that you be placed on the callout. To be placed on the callout, submit a written request to the Chaplain.

Religious Property

Personal religious property may be ordered through a special purpose order (SPO). Personal religious property <u>will not</u> be allowed to come from home. Religious items must be requested and approved by the Chaplain.

Religious Diet

If you wish to be considered for a religious diet, you must submit your request in writing to the Chaplain and a religious diet interview will be conducted. You will then be assigned to one of two religious diets offered in Food Service. Either the "No Flesh" option or the "Certified Food" diet.

Religious Resources

A large number of religious books, audio tapes, and video tapes are available. You can view videos in the chapel on your leisure time. However, you cannot view video tapes when you are expected to be on work detail. Musical instruments are used for religious worship and practice only.

Religious Visits by Clergy

If you desire, you may designate one individual on your visiting list as your minister of record (MOR) by submitting a request to the institution's Chaplain. This request must include contact information for the MOR. An approved MOR will not count against the maximum number of visitors you are allowed to have on your visiting list and may visit during normal visiting hours. Arrangements for visits by a MOR on dates you are not otherwise approved to receive a visit require the Chaplain's approval two weeks prior to that expected visit. The facility's religious program tries to assist you in your spiritual growth and development.

HINT

Try to continue your faith while incarcerated. You can use the added comfort from your religious community. The Christian Brotherhood, for example, provides hygiene products, toothpaste, shower shoes, and soap for their members upon arrival.

CHAPTER 10

Recreation

Your facility's recreation department offers leisure, wellness and structured programs designed to give every inmate an opportunity to participate. The following is a list of general programs.

Leisure Activities
Stationary bike riding, bocce ball, horseshoes, tabletop games, pool, ping pong, and weight lifting.

Arts and Crafts
Beading, crocheting, drawing, painting, leather shop, origami

Hours of operation vary per institutional staffing. Anyone interested in joining the Arts and Crafts Program must see the Recreation Department to fill out the necessary paperwork to get into the program. You can request an assigned locker in Hobby Craft if one is available. In your locker, you can keep all your art/hobby supplies.

Photo Shoots
Cameras are not permitted inside the prison. If you want pictures with family, friends or your boys you must sign up for photo shoot. Remember all photographs will get checked by CO's to make sure no gang signs or dirty shit. If you do any of those things they will come get you and throw you in the SHU. The Recreational Department will coordinate inmate photo shoots. Tickets for the photo shoots

must be purchased through commissary. Check your institution's available photo shoot times.

Wellness Program
CORE training, fitness training, ISSA correspondence courses, spinning, and yoga.

ACE Courses – Adult Continuing Education
Beginner acoustic guitar class, Salsa, and beginner crochet.

Structured Leagues
Spring/Summer basketball, bocce ball, horseshoes, volleyball, soccer, and softball. Fall/Winter chess, dominos, flag football, ping pong, pinochle, spades, and pool.

Throughout the year, the Recreation Department posts flyers that keep the inmate population informed of upcoming league play. If you wish to participate in any activities you must pay attention to the flyers and inmate bulletin boards and follow sign-up procedures and deadlines for the league startup.

Holiday Events and Tournaments
Each holiday will have special events and tournaments. Winners will receive prizes, usually commissary goodies in a special bag.

CHAPTER 11

Health Services Department

Categories of Care

The BOP Assigns Medical Problems to One of Five Categories of Care:

- Medically Necessary Acute or Emergent – A condition that if not immediately treated is life threatening, likely to cause blindness, or loss of function.

- Medically Necessary Non-Emergent – A condition that, if untreated, will result in premature death, or interfere with the possibility of later repair; or creates a level of pain or discomfort which impairs the ability to conduct activities of daily living.

- Medically Acceptable Not Always Necessary – Medical conditions whose treatment may be delayed without jeopardizing the life, sight, or bodily function of the patient.

- Limited Medical Value – Medical conditions in which treatment provides little or no medical value, are not likely to provide long gain, or are expressly for the inmate's convenience.

- Extraordinary – Medical interventions are extraordinary if they affect the life of another individual, such as organ transplants or are considered investigational in nature.

Triage

Triage determines what category of care a patient should be placed in. The purpose of triage is to make sure that truly urgent conditions are given priority treatment. During triage, the following will occur: The inmate will provide a brief history by completing the Chronological Record of Medical Care Form (Sick Call Form), vital signs will be taken and an appointment will be scheduled within a time frame appropriate for the inmate's medical need. If no follow up is warranted, the inmate will be advised of other options (i.e. what to buy over the counter medications at the commissary to alleviate that ailment).

Scope of Services

The BOP will treat all medically necessary emergent and non-emergent conditions.

Medical problems falling within the medically acceptable not always necessary category are essentially elective procedures. These procedures require approval of institution's Utilization Review Committee. The Committee considers such factors as: the risks and benefits of the treatment, available financial resources, available medical consultant resources, and the effect the intervention is likely to have on the inmate's ability to conduct activities of daily living.

Medical problems falling within the limited medical value or extraordinary categories not ordinarily treated by the BOP.

Consultants and Referrals

All care that is provided by the BOP will be consistent with community standards. When available and required, community consultants will be contracted for commonly needed services including cardiology, dermatology, endocrinology, general surgery, ophthalmology, optometry, orthopedics, psychiatry, radiology, and urology. Additionally, patients may also be referred to the BOP's medical referral centers (Fort Devins, Butner, Lexington, Springfield, and all FCIs).

Obtaining Health Care

Your ID card must be brought each time you go to Health Services. You must bring your ID picture card and verify your ID number. This ensures compliance with the double check ID system.

Out-of-Bounds

Inmates should not be in the Health Services area unless they have an appointment or scheduled callout, have obtained detail supervisor or unit officer approval, or are making use of the time period set aside for sick call sign-up or pill line.

HINT

Inmates who come by Health Services without prior approval are considered out-of-bounds and may receive an incident report.

Emergency Care

All emergencies or injuries will be screened for priority of treatment. Appropriate medical care will be provided by institutional health services staff.

Medical treatment on evenings, mornings, weekends, and Federal holidays is limited to treatment of acute problems only. Treatment needs will be determined by the medical staff. Access to emergency medical care is obtained by notifying any staff member or activation of the inmate distress system. Any emergency or injury must be reported to BOP staff immediately.

Questions regarding requests for medical care, dental care, sick call, lab results, X-ray results and eye glasses, etc. require the completion of the Chronological Record of Medical Care (Sick Call) Form. These forms are located in a rack in the Health Services facilities. The forms must be turned in during sick call times which are from 6:30 to 6:45 on Monday, Tuesday, Thursday, and Friday. You can ask questions about your medical problems of the Physician's Assistant (PA). The PA may choose to have you come back at a later date, so always check the daily callout schedule for your medical appointments. A sick call appointment requires a two dollar co-pay fee from your commissary account.

Dental Sick Call

This is for emergency care only, such as toothaches, abscesses, temporary fillings, etc. All routine appointments will be scheduled on the institution's callout.

Physical Examinations

All new commitments to the Federal BOP system will be scheduled for a complete physical examination, mandatory within 14 days of their arrival at the institution. This examination may include laboratory studies, hearing and sight screening, medical history, and physical examination. A dental examination will be completed within 30 days of an inmate's arrival. All inmates under the age of 50 are entitled to a routine physical every 2 years. Those inmates age 50 and over are entitled to one per year. These examinations include electrocardiograms, rectal probe, vision testing, blood work analysis, and other tests deemed necessary by medical staff.

Annual Immunizations/Screening

All inmates will be scheduled for tuberculosis testing on an annual basis. During influenza season, inmates will have the influenza vaccination or "flu shot" available. The optional vaccination requires an inmate to submit a cop-out to the Health Services Department requesting the flu vaccination.

Pharmacy

ID card must be brought each time you come to Health services to pick up medication from the pharmacy.

Medication Pick-Up

Monday through Friday – medications prescribed during sick call can be picked up at either 12:00 to 12:30 or 3:00 to 3:30, depending on your facility's pill line schedule.

Pill Line Times – Vary Per Institution's Staffing Schedule

For diabetics and patients taking restricted medications:

6:00 to 7:00 AM and 3:00 to 3:30 PM, Monday through Friday

7:00 to 8:00 AM and 11:00 to 11:30 AM Saturday, Sunday, holidays

Refills

All refills have a limited number and an expiration date. If you run out of refills, you need to see the PA for full renewal.

HINTS

Be prepared before entering prison. Document all chronic care problems and conditions.

Go to all scheduled medical callout appointments.

Stock up on OTC commissary medication in case you become sick. That way you can start treating your illness immediately. If OTC medications are not helping the average cold, flu, or pains, goes to sick call for medical attention.

Eat right and exercise daily. This is the time to get in shape, lose unwanted pounds, and improve your health. Many obese people come to prison and with the proper diet and exercise, leave much thinner, stronger, and healthier. Try to add more years to the back end of your life to make up for the years you lost being incarcerated.

Learn to love yourself before others. Not loving who you are will lead to depression, guilt, and increased stress levels.

Any pains or health abnormalities should be brought to Health Services' attention immediately. My bunkie at Ft. Dix was complaining of tightness in his upper torso for days. He never went to medical and 2 weeks later had a heart attack while walking the track. He had to have open-heart surgery. Don't listen to other inmates concerning medical problems, they are not qualified.

CHAPTER 12

Visiting Procedures

Visits at a Federal Correctional Facility will take place in a visiting room. The room has been arranged to provide for comfortable and pleasant visits. No smoking is permitted during visits. The visiting lists should be turned into your counselor as soon as possible, and is limited to family, close friends, business associates, and your attorney on record. Visits by retained and appointed attorneys in contemplation of prospective legal representation shall be permitted. The number of legal visits is dependent upon the nature of urgency of the problem involved. If you request the removal of an approved visitor (non-family member) from your visiting list, the person will most likely not be reinstated. You are responsible for notifying your visitors that they have been approved for visitation. The number of friends and non-immediate family on your visiting list cannot exceed 10. Visiting groups will be kept to a maximum of no more than 4 persons at one time.

Visitors must be properly dressed. Shorts, halter tops, and other clothing of suggestive or revealing nature will not be permitted in the visiting room. Visitors may not bring anything into the visiting room (e.g. books, games, or food of any type with the exception of baby food and diapers). There are vending machines serving food, snacks and beverages to the inmates and their visitors. Inmates may accompany their visitors to the vending area, however, they are not permitted to handle money or touch any of the vending machines or microwaves. Make sure that your visitors bring quarters and singles in a Ziploc bag. Note you cannot bring in a twenty dollar bill or higher, they will make you return it to your car. Visitors must have their license and insurance card with them when visiting a low to a high. Or they will make you leave to go get it or not proceed with the visit at all.

Children are to be well behaved and under constant parental supervision during visiting hours. If children become disruptive, your visit may be cancelled. All authorized items must be carried into the visiting room in a clear plastic bag. Visitors over the age of sixteen are required to have proof of identify and may only carry money into the visiting room which is to be used for vending machine purchases only. Each facility has a visiting schedule with days and designated visiting hours. On holidays, check for changes. Your facility will have directions to the prison from different locations. Call your visitors and inform them. Let them choose the easiest route. Hotel and motel information is also available should they be coming from a great distance and may want to stay over.

Telephone Procedures
All units have telephones available for your use. The Inmate Telephone System (ITS) allows you to make two types of telephone calls. You may place calls by a direct dialing method which is charged to your ITS debit account. You place funds in your debit account through the commissary. Additionally, the ITS will allow for collect calling. All calls are subject to monitoring and tape recording. In order to make an unmonitored phone call between an attorney and yourself, you must make this request to your unit manager. Also let your friends and family know when the call comes in, it was say "unavailable" or

"blocked". Telephones are intended for social use only and to consult with your attorney. The use of third party calling is prohibited. Any other use, such as running a business, is prohibited. Personal phone calls are limited to 15 minutes per hour. Inmates are allocated 300 minutes per month. All calls outside of that prison's area code cost 23 cents per minute; if you use 300 minutes per month the cost is sixty nine to seventy five dollars. (See phone hints for substantial savings – the money you'll be saving in the first month of your sentence pays for this book.)

All inmate phone numbers used to require a cumbersome paper trail. However, all Federal facilities now are online and require you to input the telephone numbers you desire on the computer for approval. To set up a new telephone number or email account you log on to that facility's computer base by using your register number, a PAC number (that the government assigns to each inmate), and a pin number which is also a private ID number assigned to each inmate. You enter the field by clicking on to ADD NEW CONTACT, the screen will pop-up and help guide you through the information fields. Once finished, you save the info and wait a day or so for the Feds to approve or decline that phone contact. We will touch on setting up email accounts in later chapters.

Phone Hints – Google Voice

GoogleVoice.com is a great product for your people to use. Your family can save a lot of money by setting up a Google Voice account. When you arrive at your prison find out what the local area codes in that vicinity are. Google will assign a local phone number for them. They do not have to change their original phone number. When you call the local assigned Google phone number, it will forward your call to your family's phone line. Instead of paying 23 cents per minute for a long distance call, you are only charged 6 cents per minute per call. In a month if you use 300 minutes at 23 cents per call it costs sixty nine to seventy five dollars; in a month if you 300 at 6 cents per call by using Google Voice, it costs only eighteen to twenty dollars. You save fifty one to fifty three dollars per month, which equals six hundred twelve to six hundred fifteen dollars per year. The money is better in your pocket. The first Google number is free and additional numbers cost a ten dollar one-time initial fee. Use only the numbers for Google that you use most often (i.e. wife, kids and parents). A Google Voice area code map has been provided in this book for your convenience.

Setting Up Your Telephone

Before you can make telephone calls, you have to record your voice on the ITS. This system has a voice recognition that allows your telephone call to go through only if it matches. This was installed because inmates who did not use all of their allocated phone minutes were selling their minutes to other inmates. For example, say Joe doesn't use his phone at all. He could sell his monthly minutes to Mike. Mike would give Joe the 1 or 2 phone numbers he used the most and Joe would get them approved. After approval, Joe would give Mike his PAC and register number so he can go on the phone when he wanted. The Feds found out about this and developed a system to fight this abuse, hence voice recognition. It can be a pain in the neck because sometimes your name doesn't match exactly over time. A hint to minimize this headache is when you first record your voice; either says your first or last name only, not both. If you can, it would be easier to just your first name – Jack. Less syllables and a greater chance that you can connect on the first try.

FBOP.GOV – Web Site

This is a publicly available web site of the Federal Bureau of Prisons. Your people can go on to this web site and find out where your co-defendants are being housed. All you need is that person's name. If it is a common last name (e.g. Smith), you will need his register number to pinpoint the right man. When you are in transit, the process can take up to three months to arrive at the prison you are assigned to. This destination is called your "home jail". I was in Ft. Dix, New Jersey waiting to transfer to Lewisburg Federal Camp, PA. Its three hours door to door, a nice easy straight shot, right? LOL. The BOP drove us to Brooklyn Federal Detention Center, we stayed there 4 to 6 weeks, then one morning they moved us to Canaan USP, PA. We stayed there another two weeks before finally taking a 30 minute bus ride to Lewisburg. So it took 8 weeks to go 3 hours away. So give this website to your family and friends, so that can look you up so they will know where you are going while you are still in transit.

Before I left Brooklyn FDC, my mom told me where I was going. She then could look it up and see the population and specific information pertaining to that facility. You can also have your people look and located your friends, co-defendants, or enemies. The website gives you that person's name, federal register number, and final release date. For example, say you became friends with someone at the Federal Detention Center. One of you transfers to their final destination; the other is still going to court. You can keep track of their final sentencing and see where they are going in case you want to say hello.

Mail Procedures

Outgoing Inmate Legal/Letter Mail

Outgoing mail should be placed in the depositories provided in every unit. The mail is picked up by the unit officer Monday through Friday with the exception of federal holidays. You may seal your mail prior to placing it in the depository.

The BOP retains the right to open outgoing correspondence as provided in the Correspondence Program Statement. Inmates may deliver their outgoing legal mail to a representative from the ISM Department or a Correctional Officer at the Control Center, Sunday through Thursday afternoon between the hours of 3:30 to 3:45 pm, excluding federal holidays. Inmates are responsible for filling out the return address completely on envelopes provided by the institution. If you use an envelope not provided by the institution, you are responsible for ensuring that the envelope used contains all return information listed on the envelope provided by the institution. Example:

Federal Correctional Institution

Inmate Name

Inmate Register Number

P.O. Box 2000

Fort Dix, New Jersey 08614

Incoming Inmate Special Mail and General Correspondence

The Unit Correctional Officer will distribute mail sometime after the 4:15 weekly count. All mail is to be given directly to the inmate. Inmates are not permitted to pick up another inmate's mail. Mail is not distributed on Saturdays, Sundays, and federal holidays. All general correspondence will be opened and examined by the mail room staff for contraband, unauthorized material, negotiable instruments, money, etc. Items considered contraband, unauthorized material or items that cannot be searched or examined without destruction will be returned to the sender. When incoming correspondence is received by unit staff, the inmate will be contacted and must report to one of the staff offices to sign for special mail.

It is necessary that you read the bulletin boards on a daily basis. Correspondence between confined inmates must be approved by appropriate staff at both institutions. Correspondence between inmates that was not approved will be returned to sender.

The Bureau Program Statement on correspondence identified certain types of incoming correspondence as "Special Mail" to be opened only in the presence of the inmate (i.e. legal mail). For this special handling to occur, BOP policy requires that the sender adequately mark "Special Mail Open Only in the Presence of the Inmate" or similar on the envelope. Inmates are responsible for informing correspondents who are authorized to utilize the Special Mail privilege of the requirements established by the BOP's Program Statement on Correspondence.

You are allowed to received magazines and soft cover paperback books from your family and friends. Newspapers and hardback covered publications must be sent to you directly from the publisher. You are only allowed to have 5 of each (magazines, newspapers, books, etc.) in your personal property at one time.

CHAPTER 13

Commissary

Commissary is available at all Federal facilities. Commissary is an excellent way to supplement your diet and buy things you need. You can buy a variety of food, hygiene products, and clothing. Use of commissary is a privilege, not a right. The commissary schedule is posted on the inmate bulletin board. Inmates must use their inmate account card for all commissary transactions. Inmate funds are retained by the institution in a trust fund you may withdraw money from for personal spending in the institution's commissary, for telephone usage, or other approved purposes. United States Postal Service money orders, cash, and Western Union wire transfers are applied to your account as soon as possible. All money orders and personal checks must include your committed name and register number. The fastest way to receive money is by Western Union. You can go online or call their toll-free number.

Western Union Funds   FBOP DC (wire code)

                                     Inmate Name

                                     Inmate Number

Mail Funds To   Federal Bureau of Prisons

                                     Inmate Name and Register Number

                                     P.O. Box 474701

                                     Des Moines, Iowa 50947

After you receive money in your account, you can start shopping. You have to go to commissary on your scheduled day, which is based on your 4th and 5th number of your personal Federal Inmate register number. Shopping is weekly, usually Monday through Thursday, with occasional holiday schedules when appropriate.

First Time Buyer

All institutions offer inmates a first time buyer privilege. It allows the new inmate arrival the ability to shop on the first day commissary is available. He does not have to wait for his scheduled commissary day.

For example, say that my shopping day based on my Federal register number is Tuesday and I arrive at my prison on Wednesday morning. As a first time buyer, I can shop on that Wednesday or Thursday. I do not have to wait until the following Tuesday to shop. Shopping quickly allows you to get the necessary hygiene items and food products you need for your comfort. Also, you can buy sweatpants, undergarments, and sneakers. A radio must also be purchased immediately because in prison the television volume is transferred to a radio frequency and muted. The only way you can watch television programs is by setting your radio to the designated station. SO MAKE SURE YOU HAVE MONEY IN YOUR ACCOUNT. When you first arrive at your prison, we recommend that you buy all your hygiene items. You will need shower shoes, shaving cream, shampoo, and laundry detergent. Hygiene is very important, you need to take showers every day and be careful. You will be housed with a large number of inmates who all have their own individual health issues. It is important to maintain your health and prevent contracting a sickness or infections from others. It is also good to buy a hand sanitizer to clean your hands frequently throughout the day. Your housing units are teeming with various bacteria and germs.

Commissary is a great privilege. It allows us to be comfortable and eases the stress of doing time and the pain of losing our freedom. Use your money wisely and get things you really need. Borrowing commissary items from other inmates is prohibited. LOL

A lot of inmates enter prison unhealthy, weak, or depressed. Use this time to improve your overall health. The commissary has a lot of healthy food alternatives to help correct your diet. You can also buy vitamins, protein bars, and heart-healthy snacks. Try to stay away from the sugar laden, high calorie snacks and beverages. We have included a few different commissary lists so you can see how many great things there are available. You can buy one book of stamps from commissary. It will not come off your spending limit. In prison, we do not have the luxury of going to good doctors and medicine is limited. However, we have included a list of over the counter medications that are available for common illnesses and ailments. We hope you find this chart useful and are sure you will be referring to it frequently.

Acne

Clearasil Cream with Benzoyl Peroxide

Allergies

Chlorphenamine Maleate Allergy Tabs

Arthritis

Aspirin 325 mgs

Acetaminophen Regular Strength

Ibuprofen Tabs 200 mgs

Muscle Rub Cream

Athletes Foot

Tolnaftate 1% cream

Anti-Fungal Powder

Back Pain

Aspirin 325 mgs

Acetaminophen Regular Strength

Ibuprofen Tabs 200 mgs

Muscle Rub Cream

Cold

Chlorphenamine Maleate Allergy Tabs

Saline Nasal Spray

Aspirin 325 mgs

Acetaminophen Regular Strength

Constipation

Fiber Powder

Milk of Magnesia

Cough

Halls Mentholyptus Cough Drops

Siltussin DM

Cuts

Band-Aids

Headache

Aspirin 325 mgs

Acetaminophen Regular Strength

Ibuprofen Tabs 200 mgs

Heart Burn

Rolaids

Tums Tablets

Antacid/Anti-gas (Mylanta)

Hemorrhoids

Hemorrhoids ointment

Jock Itch

Tolnaftate 1% cream

Muscle Aches

Aspirin 325 mgs

Acetaminophen Regular Strength

Ibuprofen Tabs 200 mgs

Muscle Rub Cream

Orthotics

Tri-comfort shoe insert

All-purpose insole

Knee wrap with compression control

Straps

Athletic supporter

Razor Bumps

Hydrocortisone cream 1%

Shampoo

Suave Dandruff shampoo

Sulfer 8 Dandruff shampoo

Skin Care

Skin Tone cream Alpha and Beta Hydroxy

Acids

Lac- Hydrin 5%

Cocoa butter lotion

Cocoa butter stick

Petroleum jelly

Suave head and body lotion with Aloe

Noxzema facial cream

Sun Burn

Moisturizing Sun Block SPF 30

These products are commonly used for certain medical ailments and carried by the commissary in most Federal facilities.

Commissary Tips

Commissary is a very important component when serving your time. Spend your money wisely. If you are on a budget, try to stock up on personal hygiene products because the Feds are always required to feed you three meals a day no matter what. Also in the beginning, you need to buy your athletic wear. Sweatpants, tee shirts, sneakers, underwear, and a radio are important. Buy a combination lock and remember to have it locked at all times when you are not near it. People can get lazy and before you know it, you are robbed by druggies or people who accumulated debts without the ability to repay them. Commissary is like AMEX, it is accepted everywhere. We don't have money in prison so we use commissary to barter for things we want. This can include extra food from the kitchen or items that an inmate from another prison has that you now want.

Budget accordingly. Do you want to shop weekly, bi-weekly, or once a month? I like to shop every two weeks I have someone that sends me money on the 1st and 15th of each month. The first thing I do is put a specific amount of money on the phone. Then I buy my food and beverage items based on their importance to me. I like to drink a lot of coffee; therefore I always buy enough coffee, creamer and sugar to cover my daily needs until I go to commissary again. I always have enough soap and skin cream to carry me for a month. Also, the Federal system has recently introduced MP3 players in the commissary. They cost sixty nine to seventy dollars and you can download a large selection of songs from the facility's computers after your MP3 is validated. The song costs vary from 75 cents to two dollars for the more popular selections. MP3s are great because you can listen to your favorite music while exercising or hanging out.

Finally, my final tip would be for you to take good care of your personal belongings so they last while you are serving time. We don't have the luxury of storing a lot of items and our financial resources are limited. Also, remember you are living with strangers who are criminals. Be careful, always lock your locker and don't leave things that have value sit out in a public area where they can be taken in the blink of an eye.

First Time Buyers List

- Shower Shoes
- Toothpaste
- Toothbrush holder
- Soups
- Soap
- Shampoo
- Book of Stamps

- Lock
- Toothbrush
- Bowl
- Drinking Mug
- Soap Dish
- Deodorant
- Mackerels

Remember that shower shoes and a lock for your locker are the most important items you need. Envelopes are free, just ask your counselors.

You will need to have about sixty to seventy dollars for this first time buy.

CHAPTER 14

Trust Fund Limited Inmate Computer System (TRULINCS)

Inmates may be approved for access to the electronic messaging system. Inmates who elect to participate in the program will pay all program fees. The BOP will withdraw all required fees directly from the inmate's Deposit Fund Account.

Inmates must submit a completed inmate agreement for participation in TRULINCS Electronic Messaging Program Form (BP-A0934-052) through your correctional counselor. TRULINCS services include: public messaging, viewing/printing personal account transactions, BP 199 Fund withdrawals, list management for phone, email and postal addresses. Also electronic law library which can be helpful with your legal work.

An inmate's contact list may have up to 100 contacts, inclusive of 30 email addresses, 30 telephone numbers and 40 mailing addresses. Inmates who add attorneys on the email contact list do so with the understanding that all emails are subject to monitoring. Inmates who have transferred in from another BOP institution will have TRULINCS access generally within a day, as their funds and TRULINCS's list transfers with them.

Access

Access to TRULINCS is provided by terminals located in the unit and are available during the hours of operation, which are 6:00 AM to 10:00 PM seven days per week, inclusive of holidays. Inmates may purchase TRULINCS session time at the rate of 5 cents per unit. Messaging is billed as one TRU-Unit per minute of session time. Inmates may purchase 40, 100, 200, 300, and 600 TRU-Units at once, which are immediately deducted from their commissary account. Printing is billed as three TRU-Units per page (15 cents). TRULINCS is unavailable to inmates whose account balance is less than the cost of the minimum increment of minutes.

Program Participation

Participation in TRULINCS is contingent upon voluntary consent to having all incoming and outgoing electronic messages, transactional data and other activities monitored by BOP staff. In the event the TRULINCS program privilege is abused, access may be limited or denied and will be subject to disciplinary action and/or criminal prosecution. Electronic messages which would jeopardize the safety, security, orderly operation of the institution or the protection of the public and staff may be rejected or blocked.

Restrictions

Inmates on any type of restriction (phone, commissary, messaging, visiting) from another institution will continue to be on restriction for the duration of the sanction.

Miscellaneous Information

Each inmate will be required to key their register number, PAC number, and TRUFAC's pin number to enter the system. Inmates will not have access to the Internet nor will they be able to receive pictures or any other attachments. The delivery of all incoming and outgoing messages is delayed by a minimum of one hour. Inmates are limited to a 30 minute session for messaging and a 30 minute period between sessions. Inmates will be billed at 1 TRU Unit = 5 cents per minute for messaging. When an inmate enters an email address on their contact list, TRULINCS sends a system generated message to the contact giving them the opportunity to accept or reject the email contact with the inmate prior to receiving any messages from the inmate. If a positive response is received, the inmate can begin exchanging electronic messages with the contact. Conversely, if a contact rejects TRULINCS participation, the inmate is blocked from sending any messages to that email address. Your friends and family have 10 days to accept your invitation, if they fail to accept in the time given, then you have to resend it to them.

Deposits

In order to utilize the program, it is necessary for inmates to purchase TRULINCS Units. Once an inmate does so, this money can only be put back into his commissary account under these circumstances: 1) release from BOP custody; 2) an inmate on email restriction for more than 30 days can request in writing that his TRULINCS balance be returned to his commissary account (a one-time transfer for the entire balance); and 3) a rare or unusual circumstance deemed appropriate by the Warden with approval in writing. This is also a one-time transfer for the entire balance.

Usage

TRULINCS stations are located in each unit. Each inmate will be allowed a maximum TRULINCS session of 30 minutes for email and 120 minutes for the Electronic Law Library access in the education department. An automatic logout will occur after those time periods are reached. Inmates will wait 30 minutes between TRULINC's sessions. Inmate use is conducted on a first-come, first-served basis. Only one inmate will be permitted to congregate near the TRULINC's area unless they are using it. The use of another inmate's email/contact list is prohibited and will result in a disciplinary shot. A banner notified the participant of consent on screen to remind the inmates of their voluntary use of the system acknowledging that the BOP has full access to all contents. In a likewise manner, all outside recipients of messaging are informed that by being active on the contact list, they are consenting to BOP monitoring and compliance with program rules and procedures. Inmates are responsible for their use of TRULINCS. They are expected to conduct themselves in a responsible manner and respect other inmates. The use of TRULINCS will not interfere with the institution's schedule, program, work assignments, or counts. When a count or census is conducted, all inmates using a workstation will terminate their session immediately. During institution emergencies, use of TRULINCS will be terminated. Inmates may access any correspondence sent or received within a 20 day timeframe. Once a message is 20 days old, it is automatically purged from the system. Inmates are not permitted to place contract staff, victims, witnesses or law enforcement officers on their contact list. Attorneys or other legal contacts may be placed on an inmate contact list knowing that all exchanges will be subject to monitoring. Inmates in Special Housing Units that are assigned to administrative detention or disciplinary segregation status will only have law library access available.

Classification and Public Safety Factor (PSF)

An inmate's exclusion from program participation must be determined on an individual basis and not on a standardized history of past convictions. Nor does the existence of a PSF automatically exempt an inmate from electronic messaging. Each case should be reviewed for underlying conduct that would prohibit them from having TRULINCS access, such as protection of the public, staff, threat of security, and interference with the safe, orderly operation of the institution. Inmates determined unsuitable to have access to the program shall receive a written explanation of the decision.

Prohibited Acts/Suspensions

Violation of any of the rules regarding the use of TRULINCS is cause for disciplinary action and the possible revocation and restructuring of messaging privileges as imposed by the DHO or UDC. Correspondence concerning illegal activities, either inside or outside of the facility may lead to criminal prosecution or a disciplinary shot.

Electronic Law Library

Inmates will have access to the electronic law library utilizing the TRULINCS system. Inmates are limited to a one hour session for this access, with a 30 minute period between sessions.

Print Services

Inmates will be permitted to utilize the TRULINCS system to print inmates account statements, TRUPHONE lists, electronic law library material, email messages, BP-199 account withdrawal forms. They will be charged 3 TRU-Units, or 15 cents per page.

Setting up the Computer

After the first day or two, your counselor will give you your ID register number, PAC account number and your personal PIN number. Memorize these numbers because you must input them in that order. Each number identifies you as the user and allows you to access and go online with TRULINCS. After you are online, go to ADD NEW CONTACT option and click on it. A screen will appear that will ask you to input the new contact information and whether they will be email, phone, mailing contacts, or all three. Input the necessary information for each individual contact. After you complete everything, save and send for approval. It usually takes one day for phone approval and two days for email approval. You must write down a list of phone numbers, addresses and emails that you want to have access to and mail them to yourself the day before you self surrender. Also, the computer has your commissary, telephone and TRULINCS balance. Very Important: When asking your friends and family for their email, explain to them that once you put them on your list for approval, an invitation from the BOP will be sent to them. Once they accept your BOP email invitation, the email address will show on the computer top left and state you have a new contact. You must email them first and tell them that when they receive the notice, it is not like normal email where it tells you that you have a new message. It will NOT be in their Inbox. They have to go on the CORRLINKS website and the email you sent them will be there. If you forget to tell them this, they won't be responding to your emails because they won't know where to retrieve them.

CHAPTER 15

Respect

In prison, this 7 letter word becomes very important and pivotal in allowing you to serve your Federal sentence with ease, comfort, and less drama. I have seen many problems arise because one inmate disrespected another inmate. These confrontations have led to fights, serious injuries, and transfers to tougher institutions after they received a shot for fighting and are sent to the SHU.

Always be respectful. Don't cut any lines, it does not matter what the circumstances are. Once you cut a line, you can count on a slick dude cursing you out loud. Now, how are you going to handle that? If he says something really bad, you have no choice but to rebut him or knock him out. At Fort Dix, there are 5,000 inmates and some people always try to cut the long chow lines. This is stupid; you are all going to eat. The pill lines are also long. So you either wait on the long line, or just sit down until the lines die down. I prefer to wait to the end if I can't get on line when it first starts. Believe me; in prison you have lines for chow, commissary, laundry, medication, and to use the damn bathroom. Be patient and respect the line. You will eventually get there.

Do not be a television hawk. You just arrived at your "home jail". The TV programming at the facility is already set and stored. Don't get there and start switching channels like you're King Farouk. Respect the programming selected and only if no one is watching anything of interest can you select a program for viewing. If there are a couple of guys in the TV room, see what they are looking to watch. If nothing is requested, ask permission to change the channel to something that interests you. Be polite. I have seen so many fights over the TV. It's not worth it.

Don't take anything that does not belong to you. I don't care if a cup has been on the card table for 2 days unclaimed. Leave it alone, because you will not be able to handle the tirade when that dude finally realizes it's missing and remembers to go get it.

Never put yourself in a position of drama. Be respectful at all times. In the showers, bathrooms, and by the microwaves, clean up after yourself. Even though there are orderlies, they aren't your mama. Another inmate following your mess will bitch and moan, guaranteed. Remember, to get respect you have to give respect.

Don't forget the courtesy flush. When you are pooping, start flushing. Don't wait to finish pooping; other people who are in the bathroom or cell with you do not need to smell it.

Another annoying habit people have in prison is listening to other people's conversations. This is called "ear hustling". This could lead to a bloody nose or black eye. Please remember not to listen to other peoples' conversations or interrupt people while they are talking. Say Jim is talking to Chaz, and you need to talk to Chaz, wait until Jim and Chaz are finished, do not interrupt their conversation or listen to what they're saying. It does not concern you, so just wait until Chaz is finished before approaching him. Also, do not be loud when people are on the phone. They might be talking about something and can't hear what they are saying because you and your friends are laughing and horsing around. You wouldn't like it if you were on the phone and couldn't carry on a conversation because someone was rapping out loud.

If you are in a two man cell or cubicle, leave the cube when your bunkie gets out of the shower. A little privacy would be appreciated while he is applying skin lotions and getting dressed. Also, do not peek in cells, cubes or rooms if you are not looking for the person in that cube. It is rude and people might think you're casing their room looking to steal something.

Remember; always use your right hand when giving someone a pound. To use your left hand or shake someone's hand with a glove on is disrespectful.

Don't look at other people's mail and make sure your rip and shred the return address on yours so people don't write to your friends or family.

Finally, at 10:30 pm, it is lights out and quiet time begins. If you want to read after that, buy a book light.

If you are in a two man room or cell, you and your bunkie must come to an agreement over some of the issues discussed above. Be real, my friend, and remember R-E-S-P-E-C-T spells respect!!

CHAPTER 16

Maintaining Personal Hygiene and Avoiding Diseases

This chapter is very important. Due to the large amount of people in your unit, your personal hygiene care is vital. There are many third world foreigners in the Federal system. Many of them have poor hygiene and carry many diseases due to either poor health care, or poor health care facilities and personnel. For example, a lot of Dominicans get infected with tape worms. My bunkie told me stories of improper refrigeration and lack of daily meat inspections that resulted in his people contracting tapeworms.

Bathroom

When you arrive at your final prison destination, try to get a spray bottle. They have disinfectant available to the orderlies. You can usually buy a spray bottle for two to three MACs. If you can't buy one once you arrive, ask one of your roommates to use theirs. When you enter the bathroom stall, completely spray the toilet with the disinfectant. Wipe the seat, and do your business. If you can't find any disinfectant, wipe the bowl down and put your shower shoes on the seat, and sit on top of them so your ass never touches the seat. Also, remember if you trim your beard or get a haircut in the bathroom, you must clean up after yourself. If not, people will complain and bitch at you. It becomes a problem, so always remember that you are still responsible for your own messes even though you have bathroom orderlies assigned to clean the bathroom facilities daily.

TIP

Always wash your hands upon leaving the bathroom. Medical professionals inform us that by washing our hands a few times a day, we can limit the germs and bacteria we might come in contact with. Always wash your hands before eating, as well.

Showers

The most important thing I can mention in this section is to have/ borrow shower shoes before entering the shower. You are in prison; a lot of the inmates are Vikings. They will piss, shit, and jerk-off their Johnson in the shower. Also, a lot of these individuals have nail fungus and athlete's foot. If you ever had these problems before, you know how difficult it is to cure these common foot ailments. When you first arrive in prison, go see the Christian Brothers, they usually have a healthcare package which includes toothpaste, toothbrush, shower shoes, and soap. You will be asked to replace the items when you go to commissary. If you can't do a first time buyer commissary shop, wait until you go to commissary before you take a shower, and buy the shower shoes first. Remember, our feet and hands come into contact with a lot of germs, bacteria and infectious diseases. If you drop something in the shower, leave it, even if it is brand new. You don't want to take a chance of catching something if you use it again. Take extra care of your hands and feet to avoid problems down the road.

Also, always remember to wear your gym shorts or pants to the shower. Never go to the showers with your boxers. It is a respect thing and you should know homosexuality runs rampant in prisons.

Do not pick up personal belongings of others. Lots of time people will forget their boxers, shampoo, towels, mirrors, and soap in the bathroom or by the shower stalls. Do not be a thief and take the already used products. It's embarrassing to be caught and shows a lack of respect. My friend Tommy at FCI Fort Dix forgot his shampoo in the shower. When he noticed it was missing, he went back. Someone had stolen his shampoo within 3 minutes of leaving the shower stall. The next day Tommy found an empty shower bottle and pissed in it. He put it in the shower stall and left. Five minutes later it was missing. I wish I could have seen the look on the face of the person who took the bottle when he actually used it. So remember, if you step into the shower and there is something in it, just put it next to the shower so the right person can reclaim it.

In the BOP, they have one man showers. I know that was one of your biggest fears. Lots of time I joke with guys and tell them they have gang showers. When they finally go to their destination and see that they are single showers, we all have a good laugh. Showers are on a first come, first served basis. If all the showers are taken, people reserve the next one by placing a chair in line of the shower they wish to use. When that person is finished, they can go in. When possible, bring your chair to the shower to place your clean clothes, towel, soap, and shampoo on top of it. Some showers do not have adequate hooks and shelves. Remember we are not at the Holiday Inn. When you are done with your shower, don't forget to take all your personal belongings with you any garbage (soap wrapper, empty shampoo bottles) with you. Respect others as you would want to be respected. Shower every day, do not be the person everyone is talking about. If you intend to work out either early in the morning or late at night, shower immediately after as well. In the summer, you may have to shower twice daily. However, it is better to be fresh and clean then offensive to others. In prison, guys who are dirty or smell have problems. People will give them an initial warning to adhere to. If they do not listen, problems arise; they may be beaten up, thrown out of the room, or have their personal belongings stolen.

HINTS

Buy shower shoes ASAP. Never enter any shower barefoot

Clean the bathroom stall with a lot of disinfectant

Wash your hands frequently

Don't be a toiletries thief

Bring back all of your toiletries after a shower or shave. If you leave your mirror in the bathroom, it will be missing within 5 minutes.

Respect others; don't walk around naked before or after a shower.

CHAPTER 17

Personal Appearance

It is the responsibility of each inmate to keep himself clean and well-groomed at all times. The institution provides bathroom facilities for daily showering, and issues toilet paper, toothbrush, soap, comb, and disposable razor.

Inmate Dress Code

Each inmate is responsible to present himself in a clean, acceptable manner of dress in all areas of the institution. Inmates are permitted to select the hairstyle of their choice, but maintain cleanliness and dress in keeping with standards and the security, good order, and discipline of the institution. All religious headgear must be approved by one of the chaplains.

All inmates will be fully dressed within 30 minutes after leaving their beds in the morning. Inmates will have shirts buttoned and tucked inside their pants and their belts buckled. Inmates will either be in their work uniform (Monday – Friday during working hours) or their recreational attire.

Days Off

Inmates will not be allowed to lounge around in the unit in pajamas or robes. Inmates in the unit with scheduled days off will be dressed in an appropriate inmate uniform, shorts and shirt, or sweats. Any clothing that has been altered is considered contraband. During periods of movement on work days, the full inmate uniform must be worn.

Shirts

Inmates will be expected to button their shirts but can leave the two top buttons unbuttoned. All shirts will be tucked in. The shirt may be removed from the body when participating in athletic events. Shirts may not be worn with collar turned up or rolled over. Inmates may not wear shirts with one sleeve rolled up and one sleeve rolled down. Sleeveless shirts will not be worn in the dining hall.

Undergarments

No undershorts or underwear will be worn as an outer garment or displayed on the outside of clothing at any time. Long sleeve thermals are not to be worn under khaki short sleeve shirts during the work day.

Tee-Shirts

Institution tee-shirts may be worn as an outer garment work shirt out on work details (e.g. landscaping). On all details, the khaki shirt will be worn. On details with unique safety considerations, certain equipment and clothing requirements will be mandated.

Pants

Inmates are required to wear their pants around the waist with pants legs extended to the ankle and properly hemmed. Inmates may not tuck their pants legs inside their shoes or socks. Inmates are required to wear properly fitted pants. They cannot pleat the waist area or wear pants with the pockets pulled inside out.

Footwear

All inmates are required to wear steel-toed safety boots at work.

Athletic Gear

Athletic clothing, shorts, and sweat suits may be worn to the evening meal on regular work days, to all meals on weekends and holidays, to the recreational units, and in the housing units. When in the recreation yard, a tee-shirt or approved shirt must be worn. Inmates can write their name and register number on personal athletic clothing. If so, the inmate must mark his athletic tops on the left front breast, and the athletic pants on the left front at waist level, using black ink only. Any other color and that clothing will be considered contraband and will be confiscated. (Gangs usually ride colors, e.g. Bloods-red, Crips-blue)

Headgear

Only headgear issued by the institution, sold in the commissary, or approved by religious services is authorized.

Altered Clothing

Any personal clothing that is pegged, tapered, dyed, fitted, marked or otherwise altered from the original manufactured condition will be considered contraband and confiscated.

Food Service Issued Clothing

Food Service "whites" or smocks are authorized for food service workers only and worn only in the dining hall during their working hours and for educational classes. All other areas are prohibited.

Food Service

All meals at your FCI facility are served cafeteria style at the food service building.

Normal Serving Times Weekdays

Breakfast	6:00 to 7:00 AM
Lunch	10:30 AM to finish
Dinner	4:30 PM to finish

Normal Serving Times Weekends and Holidays

Breakfast	6:30 to 7:30 AM
Brunch	10:30 to 11:30 AM
Dinner	4:30 PM to finish

Rotation

UNICOR is always first, followed by facilities, then each unit is called based on that weeks' unit placement.

Meal Attire

For lunch, Monday through Friday, you must wear your issued work clothing. For breakfast and dinner and all meals on Saturday, Sunday, and Federal holidays, you may wear non-issued clothing (sweatpants, tee-shirts, and shorts) with the exception of approved clothing. No hats are to be worn in the dining room, and shirt tails must be tucked in. Flip flops/shower shoes are prohibited. Sleeveless shirts are never authorized to be worn in food service. Radios, newspapers, magazines, books, etc. are prohibited. No food of any kind is to be brought into food service for preparation or consumption. Also, the only food that is permitted to be taken out of food service is one piece of fresh fruit.

The only inmates permitted to eat at early "short line" are those working in food services or those having prior approval by the Warden. An example would be commissary and education workers who need to eat earlier so they can go to work.

Main Line

All the respective heads of the different facility areas and the Warden are available to hear any of your grievances with staff or any other problem you might have every day at lunch. Finish your meal and politely go to the person you may want to see. I would advise you to try to solve the problem with that area first before you go to the Warden or the Assistant Warden. For example, I was having a problem with my leg. I had a skin boil that kept recurring, and my doctor at Fort Dix thought it would heal itself. After two months of constant pain and bloody sheets and clothing, I spoke to the head of Health Services at Main Line. I politely explained what I was going through and he set up an appointment with an outside surgeon to cut the entire skin boil off my thigh so the infection would heal. I don't really like to go over anyone's head or violate the "chain of command", but sometimes these BOP people refuse to help you and then the only logical next step other than filling out a BP-8 and formally "ratting out" the staff person whose ineffectiveness is frustrating, is to vent your problem at the Main Line.

A list of contact offices of the BOP throughout the United States is found after this paragraph. If you have a problem, you must always contact the regional office that handles your facility. For example, if a Fort Dix inmate had a problem or grievance he would write to the Northeast Regional Office in Philadelphia, Pennsylvania.

U.S. Department of Justice

Office of the Inspector General

950 Pennsylvania Avenue, NW, Suite 4322

Washington, DC 20530-0001

Central Office

Federal Bureau of Prisons

320 W. First Street, N.W.

Washington, DC 20534

Mid-Atlantic Regional Office

302 Sentinal Drive, Suite 200

Annapolis Junction, MD 20701

North Central Regional Office

Gateway Complex Tower II, 8th Floor

400 State Avenue

Kansas City, Kansas 66101-2492

Northeast Regional Office

US Customs House, 7th Floor

2nd and Chestnut Streets

Philadelphia, PA 19106

South Central Regional Office

4211 Cedar Springs Road, Suite 300

Dallas, TX 72519

Southeast Regional Office

3800 North Camp Creek Parkway, SW

Building 2000

Atlanta, GA 30331-5099

Western Regional Office

7338 Shoreline Drive

Stockton, CA 95219

CHAPTER 18

Sexual Offender – "Chomo" – "Pedophile"

Okay, I guess the gig is up. You have been arrested for child pornography, distribution of children pornography, or engaging in sexual behavior with a boy or girl under eighteen years old. I wish I had some good things to tell you about doing Federal time under these circumstances. Unfortunately, that would be a lie. In the Federal system, since the 80s and 90s, inmates primarily cared if the new guy was a rat or gay. Since 2000, the first thing people are concerned about is if the new guy is a pedophile. Being a rat is still bad, but it looms in 2nd place behind sexual predatory child offenders. At Fort Dix, which is only a low, pedophiles and chomos are abused daily. They are beaten up at night while they are sleeping. They are constantly getting their lockers robbed and not allowed certain privileges that other inmates are afforded. For example, once you enter your home jail, your roommates or cellies will ask you what your charges are. It does not pay to lie to them. Be truthful, humble and try to soften the actual details of the crime you committed. Nowadays, because of the advancement of social and public media, inmates could call their family or pop-on a cell phone that they may have and process a personal legal inquiry as to why you have been imprisoned. If you lie and they find out, your life will be miserable. If you are somewhat humble, truthful, and show remorse for the things you did, they may allow you to serve your time with minimal problems. In 2010, one inmate at Fort Dix was fighting with a pedophile and accidently pushed him down the stairs. That pedophile was killed and that federal inmate who pushed him had to cop-out to a manslaughter charge that carried another 14 to 16 years when he was only serving a 27 month sentence to begin with.

HINTS

If you are considered "sexual offender status" always be careful. Adhere to the demands your roommates or other inmates at the facility have placed on you. Keep a low, low profile. As a pedophile in Federal custody, you have no rights according to your peers. You can't run the televisions, phones, or sit at certain food tables in the kitchen. Keep to yourself, the less people you know or chill with, will allow you a greater change of fitting in. Do not hang out with the pedophile gang. At the Lows, pedophiles hang out with pedophiles, gays hang out with gays, and rats hang out with rats. You want to minimize the circumstances of your case; you don't want to draw attention to yourself by hanging out with other known pedophiles, particularly if some of the guys you stay with sexually assaulted minors. The other inmates always talk and point out "chomos" as they travel around the compound. Please look at the Hints at the end of the chapter. If you feel that at any time your safety is threatened, do not hesitate to go to the Lieutenant's office and ask to be placed in protective custody. Sometimes a transfer is warranted.

Keep a tight circle – do not hang out with known pedophiles

Be humble and remorseful about your crimes

Keep your locker locked whenever leaving the room or cell

Adhere to in-jail "pedophile restrictions"

Only buy enough commissaries to last a week. If you stock up, you increase your chances of being robbed.

CHAPTER 19

Shakedowns/Contraband

Searches

Any staff member may search your living quarters to retrieve contraband. It is not necessary for you to be present. Your property and areas will be left in the same general condition as found. The searches will be unannounced and conducted in a random manner. Also, you are subject to personal searches when staff determines that it is appropriate. On occasion, dogs trained to detect drugs and other contraband items will aid in searches.

Contraband

Contraband is defined as any item not issued to you by the institution, received through proper channels, or purchased through the commissary. This includes food items from the dining room with the exception of one piece of fruit or diabetic snack. All items in your possession must be authorized and recorded on your Inmate Property Form or commissary receipt. You are prohibited from purchasing, giving, or receiving radios, watches, or any other item from another inmate.

Hints

During the last few years, Federal prisons, usually Low or camp facilities, have been flooded with cell phones. With modern technology, cell phones have Internet, Facebook, picture capabilities, and a million other uses. Inmates are bored and have nothing but time on their hands, so they purchase a cell phone for recreational fun and to make unmonitored phone calls. This is a security risk to the facilities staff and inmates. Also, inmates can circumvent the institution's monitored phone system. With a cell phone they can run legitimate and illegal businesses, threaten people, and plan escapes. The entire BOP is up in arms over all the cell phones entering the facilities. If you are caught on a cell phone, you will receive a serious shot, be placed in the SHU, and expect to get transferred to a facility at a higher custody level (camp to a Low, Low to a Medium, and Medium to a USP). You will also lose good time and may get a new charge if they can prove you used a phone for business purposes, or threatened the welfare of others both in and outside of the Federal system. Be very careful, it is not worth it. It may seem like fun to go on Facebook, text the ladies, receive online sex photos on your phone, or surf the Internet. However, remember the downside. Phones, drugs, alcohol, and cigarettes are serious offenses behind the fence and walls. At Fort Dix, they throw duffle bags filled with tobacco, drugs, and phones over the walls to inmates. Inmates at Fort Dix who are successful in getting a package could make twenty five thousand to thirty five thousand dollars, if not more. However, remember how severe the downside will be if you get caught. You can lose all your good conduct time, be transferred to a higher facility away from home, or incur another indictment whose charges will be consecutive to what you are now serving.

Be wise, stay on the down-low and chill. No need to increase the drama that is already in your life because of incarceration. If an extreme emergency exists when you might need to use a cell phone, use a spotter to watch for the COs and make sure that the number you call is erased from the phone after you call.

CHAPTER 20

Currency – What is It?

In prison, we are not allowed to possess US currency. We have to go back to the days when commerce was conducted using a barter system. In prison, when we want to purchase something from the kitchen or something another inmate is selling, there are a few ways to accomplish this. At Fort Dix, common currency is mackerel (mac), tuna, and stamps. Mackerels are valued at one dollar, tuna at one dollar fifty cents, and stamps vary between six and seven dollars per book. Kitchen guys for example may sell peppers and onions at one mac each. A bag of oatmeal might cost 2 tunas or about three to four dollars. You may want to buy a used radio for twenty one to twenty four dollars or three books of stamps. The final alternative is to buy something from someone by letting them choose commissary for the same value as the item you want to purchase. You can also send money to an inmate's account or family by Western Union or a Postal Money Order. However, you must be discrete.

HINT

A good thing to do when you arrive at prison is to buy macs, tuna, or stamps in bulk. A lot of people who hustle want to exchange their prison currency for money. You buy their macs and tuna at a discount and will have it when you need to buy something or pay for their services.

Lower Bunk Pass

Lower bunk assignments will be issued by medical staff only if the inmate:

- Is currently being treated for insulin dependent diabetes, or seizure;
- Has an artificial limb, fracture, or limb paralysis;
- Is age 60 or older
- Weighs in excess of 350 pounds.

Special Shoes (Soft Shoe)

Requests for special footwear (non-steel toe boots, soft shoes, etc.) will be approved only if one of the following conditions is met:

- The patient is an insulin dependent diabetic with circulatory impairment
- The patient has a deformity which prevents placement of the foot into a pair of properly fitting institution shoes.

HINT

When it is time to see the doctor, tell him you have a bad back and you go to the bathroom a lot throughout the night, and having a lower bunk pass is very important so you don't have to climb up and down all the time. Believe me, it is a pain in the ass. Also stress to the doctor that you have a lot of pain in your heels and feet. If the doctor awards you with the soft shoe pass, you are going to thank us every day. Wearing BOP issued boots is very uncomfortable as they are very heavy. You have to wear the boots all day until after 4:00 count, and then you can wear your sneakers.

HELPFUL HINTS

Personal Hints

- If you need a back scratcher, break your hanger and use the long part, works like a charm.

- To make a cheese grater, use the top of an AJAX can, make the holes a little bigger. Comes in handy.

- When cleaning your eye glasses, put a drop of dishwashing soap on each lens, rub with your fingers and then rinse off.

- If the tips of your fingers are yellowed from smoking, find sandpaper or go in between the bricks of a building and rub them hard.

- If you can quit smoking before you come in, you should. It is hard to get and a very expensive habit if you can't stop.

- Sneezing – if there isn't any tissue around, sneeze into your shirt, do the same for coughing.

- In the summer time take your blankets and lay them under your bed, it make it a lot more comfortable.

- Save the nicest outfit they give you, get it ironed and save it for visits. The same goes for either sneakers or boots, put them inside a trash bag and tie it. This way you will look sharp for your guests.

- If you can get an extra thermal top, cut the sleeve to make a hat. Cut it to size and sew the smaller end. Now you have a hat.

- When you have a medical pass and you don't have to work, post it on your locker or bed so the COs can see it and you don't mess up their count.

- If you find yourself in the SHU or in Transit, they give you very little deodorant. If needed, wet the tip of your soap bar and use that.

- Empty Pop Tart boxes or any little boxes you get are good to stick to your locker to store stuff.

- If and when you lose your string to your shorts or sweats take an ink pen with a cap, bend the string over the tip of the pen, put the cap back on tight, then slide the pen into the hole in your pants and slide it around. This will save you a bunch of time, trust me.

- Toothpaste is really good for a few things. For example, it dries out pimples and is also a really good glue to hold things once it dries.

- Orange juice is good to use as hair gel, and so is shaving cream. This is useful if your home jail doesn't stock these items.

- The elastic from your underwear can be used to make jail house sleeping blinders with a towel or old sweatpants.

- Do not reach or stand over an inmate's food.

- If you get called to go see the CO, it's a good idea to bring another inmate so he can witness that you are not ratting on someone.

- If you get a scratch on your eyeglass lens, use white toothpaste and rub it into the lens. The scratches will disappear.

- Batteries are a smoker's best friend. Wait, you'll see!

- When getting ready to eat your Crackhead Soup, the best way to break it up is to throw it flat on the floor.

- Here is where prison is crazy. You are not supposed to spit in the sink; you are to use the toilet bowl instead. But, blowing your nose in the sink is okay...crazy but true.

- When going to the bathroom, keep flushing the toilet so it doesn't stink the place up. This is a big deal, trust me.

- When emailing your friends and family, remember it takes a few hours before they can receive it or you get theirs.

- Let your friends and family know when you call them it's going to show on their phones as "unavailable".

- When walking or running around the track, go the same way everyone else is. If you going against the traffic it means you are looking for a date.

- Try not to talk about your case or personal life to other inmates. There are a lot of haters in here, and they will try to twist it somewhere down the road on you.

- Do not loan money, anything could happen in here, it's just a headache you can avoid.

- Don't be in a rush to make friends, give yourself a few weeks to assess your surroundings.

- When making a phone call you can dial the number and the code; you don't have to listen to the recording. Let the person know on the other end they only have to listen for a few seconds then press #5. They also don't have to listen to the whole message.

- When using the phone, make sure you clean it first. You will see some inmates using a sock; they slide it over the receiver so they don't pick up germs.

- If someone offers you chips or pretzels, never reach your hand into their bag. Cup your hands and they will pour some into your hand.

- When getting a new razor, rub the razor up and down your pants leg to dull the blade a bit, or it's going to cut up your face.

- When one of your friends is going home, make sure you take everything he's not taking with him. (Sneakers, hangers, shelves, long johns, etc.) If not for you, for the next inmate who needs it.

- Housing Hints

- To keep your chair from scratching the floor or making noise when sliding it on the floor, take an old pair of socks and slide them up the chair legs.

- Before you go to the commissary to buy Mackerel so you can have currency for one dollar and forty cents each, try to find someone who sells Macs for one dollar. You can save a bunch of cash this way (bookies, laundry, kitchen woks, store guys are the people to see).

- Learn some card games or chess before you come in, because everyone plays (spades, gin, casino, dominoes) and it's a great way to kill time.

- Irons can be used to heat up food, so if you come across any aluminum foil, save it.

- Razors are the best way to cut up onions and peppers, ask an inmate how to do it.

- Air freshener – take some toilet paper and fold it together, squeeze some of your roll-on deodorant on the paper, then stick the paper by the vent.

- Air vents blowing too much air – wet some toilet paper and cover the vent by throwing the paper against it. Another way is to take a sheet of paper and put toothpaste on the four corners of the page and place it over the vent.

- Fabric softener sheets are good to hang in your locker as an air freshener, cologne inserts in magazines work well too.

- Orange peels and fabric softener sheets in your sneakers work well for both you and your cellie.

- If your shower shoes rip on the top, shoe strings work well to keep them together until you can get to the commissary. Sewing works also.

- The lid on your drinking jug is going to snap off, it's just a matter of time. When it breaks off, pop a hole in both ends with a pen and feed a shoe string through the holes and tie a knot on both ends. Problem solved.

- When you have extra tape, don't throw it away. Stick it to your locker and use it as you need it.

- There are little magnets in your headsets. When the headsets break, take the magnets out and save them.

- Don't throw away any screws or bolts. They are good for holding up shelves or to hang your clothes on.

- Shaving in the shower – take your mirror and some toilet paper, wet the toilet paper and stick it to the wall, then push your mirror against the toilet paper, and the mirror will stay there.

- Ice cream containers make good pen and marker holders.

- Always rip the return address off your mail. Trust me; you will hear bad stories about that. Inmates writing your girl… it happens.

- Rubber bands are good to close potato chip bags, etc.

- When borrowing a fellow inmate's book, make sure you don't crease the top of the page so you can remember what page you are on. Respect their property.

- If you borrow something, make sure you return it as soon as possible.

- Roll up a few newspapers and put socks on each end to the size of your door. This will make a great noise blocker.

- Oatmeal boxes are good to hold your medications or spices.

- To keep your soda cold, get your bowl and fill it with ice, spin the soda on the ice and it will get very cold.

- An old ink pen is good for holding on to thread or tape. Wrap it around so it doesn't get tangled up.

- If your window is clouded, take the jelly they give you and rub it in a washcloth and apply it to the window. It will take away the stuff so you can look out the window.

- When it starts getting cold, placing your drink/milk by the window even if it doesn't open will keep it cold.

- Keep all commissary receipts in case you have to prove to them that you purchased an item. This is especially helpful when you are going from one prison to another and they don't sell the item at your new prison. If you don't have this proof of purchase, they may throw the item away.

- Take an iron, plug it in, take three rolls of toilet paper, make a stand, and put the iron on top of them with the metal part of the iron in the air. Now you have a grill.

- If you don't have laundry detergent, take a bar of soap and place it in a sock and smash it on the floor a few times. Now you have detergent.

- Peanut butter jars are really valuable to use as a jug, or to hold things in them. Here's a good trick when you're ready to clean the jar out. Rip up a newspaper, stick it into the jar, add warm water, close the lid and shake it well, then rinse it out. It's completely clean.

- If you need scotch tape, peel the label off your deodorant bottle and you now have scotch tape.

- Potato chip bags – the big ones are good to put soda and ice into, no leaking.

- Any zip lock bags – like the ones that you get with your wraps are good to store cookies and stuff like that to keep them fresh.

- Baby powder is good to keep your playing cards new. If you store your cards by placing one face up and the other face down in the storage box, they will last a long time.

- Shelves in your locker – you can tie shoe strings across your locker and place cardboard on the strings, and you have a shelf. If you are lucky enough to get shelves in your locker but there is some rust on them, you can line them with newspaper to solve the rust problem.

- Socks are good to put over your water jug to keep it from sweating all over the place.

- Dental floss is good to use as thread.

- You can rip up old shirts to make clothes lines or cleaning rags.

- The elastic from your underwear can be used to make jail house sleeping blinders with a towel or old sweatpants.

- Do not reach or stand over an inmate's food.

- Never sit on someone's bed or their chair or move their chair in the TV rooms. At the camp they will tap your shoulder and ask you to move. In the Lows, Meds, or Pens, you will get tapped on the jaw or worse. You have been warned.

- Always knock or ask to come into a room or cell.

- An empty creamer zip lock bag makes a great ice pack.

- If someone lets you borrow something like a tattoo magazine, etc. do not lend it to your friend or your neighbor or anyone else. If the guy comes back for it makes sure you have it in your possession. Never just take anything even if he's your boy because if it is not his and that person comes to get it and your friend doesn't know where it is, it could get ugly quick.

- When you are getting ready to throw away your old mirror for a new one, there is a nice size magnet on the back of the mirror; take the magnet, it comes in handy.

- If your door slams shut, take an old rag or sock and hang it over the door and tape it to the door.

- When you are not sure which batteries are not good, drop them one at a time. The ones that don't bounce high are the good ones; the ones that bounce high are trash.

- If you are going to double stuff your pillow, get a big trash bag and place them both in there and make one pillow. If you don't, there will be feathers everywhere and the COs will see them and check everyone's pillow. It is not good, trust me.

- If someone you just met asks you to get them a few things from commissary, tell them you don't have money like that, or you will be getting them something every week. Nip it in the bud right off the rip.

- When making a drink with one of the juice packets, pour the packet into your jug and add a little 190 (hot water) and spin it. Prevents staining.

- When going to the commissary to purchase more than a hundred to hundred and ten dollars, it's a good idea to bring two bags to carry your stuff. Split the commissary into two bags evenly, then tie the two bags together and throw it over your shoulder and away you go. If you think it might be too heavy for you, grab an inmate and offer him an ice cream to help carry your bags for you.

- The empty soda case makes for a pretty good garbage can, empty it often. If you get the opportunity to buy a cooler, buy it. They don't sell them on commissary anymore. They are great in the summertime but good all year to put meats or milk and eggs into. You need to make sure that you ice this stuff down before storing it.

- When handling your commissary sheet, it is a good idea to highlight everything you want.

- When going to commissary, write two lists and hand one list in. Try to look at the other one as they are passing the products through the window and check it off as it comes through the window. Once you leave that window, if they forget something you have to wait until the following week. Once you walk away from the window, there is no going back. All sales are final.

- Try not to listen to all the hoopla about 65% or getting out early. Sit back and do your time. There is a saying in here and it's very true. Think the worst, hope for the best.

Take it from me starting at the beginning of the tunnel was the darkest period in my life waiting to go in to prison. I felt like my life was over and that there was no hope for me. While I was inside I worked hard to get my GED, I went through the RDAP program I got out went through the halfway house, now I am on parole starting my life over completely. Currently I am living as a clean and sober person working harder than I ever have in my life trying to make positive changes in my life. It is not easy at all but being free is completely worth it. I have come out the other side and I see the light and all the amazing things the future holds for me. I remind you that THE MOST IMPORTANT THING IN THIS BOOK is to make sure you ask your lawyer about RDAP. If you don't, you will be kicking yourself in the ass. That I promise you...